The Ultimate Guide to College Safety

How to Protect Your Child From Online
& Offline Threats to Their Personal
Safety at College & Around Campus

By Peter J. Canavan

www.CampusSafetyUniversity.com

Published by
PJC Services, LLC
512 Northampton St.
Kingston, PA 18704
https://PJCservices.com

Attention:
Quantity discounts of this entire book or individual chapters are available to your educational institution, company or other organization at significant discount for reselling, educational purposes, subscription incentives, gifts, or fundraising campaigns. Contact *PJC Services* directly via phone or email with your requested quantity.

Manufactured in the United States of America.

Canavan, Peter J
The Ultimate Guide to College Safety: How To Protect Your Child From Online and
    Offline Threats To Their Personal Safety at College and Around Campus
Paperback: 978-1-64440-874-2
    ebook: 978-1-64440-875-9

Cover design by: PJC Services
Interior design: PJC Services
Photography by: Tom Mooney
Sparring partner: Austin Canavan

website: http://CampusSafetyUniversity.com

Disclaimer:
Although the author and publisher have made every effort to ensure that the information in this book was correct at press time, the author and publisher do not assume and hereby disclaim any liability to any party for any loss, damage, or disruption caused by errors or omissions, whether such errors or omissions result from negligence, accident, or any other cause. This book is not intended as a substitute for the medical advice of physicians. The reader should regularly consult a physician in matters relating to his/her health and particularly with respect to any symptoms that may require diagnosis or medical attention. The author and publisher advise readers to take full responsibility for their safety and know their limits. Before practicing the skills described in this book, be sure that you do not take risks beyond your level of experience, aptitude, training, and comfort level. This book is licensed for your personal enjoyment and education only and is meant to supplement, not replace, self-defense training from a qualified instructor.

For every parent who has ever worried about their child . . .

I'm sure you would agree that keeping your child safe is one of the most important responsibilities you have when raising them.

This book is the roadmap that will help your child during the next chapter of their life and beyond.

It is my sincere hope that the information presented here helps put your mind a bit more at ease as your son or daughter heads off to college.

* * *

For every college-bound student . . .

Nervous about college and what the future holds for you? Maybe you're feeling a bit overwhelmed? Stressed? This is normal! The road ahead will be tough, but rewarding, I promise you! This book will help reduce the risks to your personal safety both on-line and off-line. It will increase your overall safety awareness. It will help you develop the right mindset and attitude. It will help build your confidence. It will ultimately assist in guiding you toward more informed and safer decisions in college and beyond.

Best of luck in your future endeavors!

Stay safe!

In the Spring of 2016 it hit me like a ton of bricks. Was I really going to have a kid going to college in another year? How could this have happened so soon? My first-born son (I have three boys) would be graduating high school and preparing for the next chapter of his life. It was unsettling, not to mention it made me feel old!

Questions began to flood into my mind. Would he stay safe? Make smart decisions? Change his major? Graduate on time? Be overwhelmed with student debt? Get a job after college? Move away after graduation? Would my wife (a teacher for over 25 years) and I see him much after that? It just didn't seem real. How could this have happened to our "little boy?"

It was at that point that I became concerned. College students and their parents used to worry about getting good grades, finding a job after graduation and whether or not they would be living at home after college. However, in recent years the primary concern has been making sure that our sons and daughters stay safe at college.

I decided to do something others might consider a bit drastic. I decided to become a public safety officer at a local college. I could learn what threats existed that I may not be aware of by seeing it from the inside as a university employee. Now all I had to do was figure out what background checks and training I needed to do, submit some resumes to local colleges and get hired - all within the next six months. No pressure, right?

Now, I am a full-time computer consultant, having run my own business since 1995. Performing this job as a safety officer would require me to do it in addition to my regular career—essentially a second full-time job! Goodbye sleep! After much deliberation and discussions with my wife, we decided that the short-term sacrifice was worth it to keep kids safe.

I am also a martial arts instructor (20+ years) and teach classes to both children and adults every week. My expertise in physical self-defense, coupled with my experience keeping my clients' computers safe and secure, and now as a university public safety officer, put me in a unique position. I would compile a comprehensive safety guide that my sons (and others) could use to stay safe from all manner of online and offline threats.

I have extensively researched the problems facing today's youth, bring awareness to them, and provide comprehensive, realistic solutions for college students who face threats that generations before never did. Topics in this book include bullying & cyber-bullying, alcohol responsibility, credit card and ATM safety, dorm room security, personal boundaries, sexual and physical assault, terrorism, cyber-security, social media and cell-phone safety, active shooters and personal safety both on and off-campus. This book also contains important information about how to build confidence, maintain the proper attitude, and build various other skills to ensure success both in college and in life.

I sincerely hope that you find the following valuable and informative. Stay safe!

TABLE OF CONTENTS

Your Safety Concerns

Part 1: Defining Your Concerns

As a new college student, there are many things that are going to be new to you. If you are staying on campus, you will have to get used to doing a lot of things that you may not have done up to this point in your life. Even if you are commuting, there are a lot of adventures that await.

Some of the more obvious include getting up by yourself for class (without mom or dad prodding you up in the morning), figuring out how to do your own laundry (and not wash whites with reds), learning how to cook (on a budget), navigating campus (a completely new area to you), discovering what it's like to live with someone else (who you may not get along with), making sure your work gets done (on time), making new friends (and girlfriends/boyfriends) and so on.

There are some other not-so-obvious concerns that you will undoubtedly face during college. These include financial concerns (do you really need a credit card?), alcohol responsibility (or irresponsibility), travel concerns (going abroad for a semester or just home for the weekend), potential computer and Internet problems (cyber-security, cyber-bullying, social networking, stolen computer), dorm room security (yes, you need to keep your door locked), and personal safety threats from a variety of sources including bullies, rapists, violent attackers, terrorists and active shooters.

It would be nice if we could just say, "That won't happen to me—I'm going to a 'good' school in a 'good' city." Unfortunately,

I've got some bad news for you. In recent surveys of college campuses across the United States, so-called "better" schools and those of Ivy League caliber actually had <u>higher</u> incidents of physical assault and rape than other colleges and universities (https://www.theguardian.com/commentisfree/2014/apr/03/ivy -league-harvard-anonymous-sexual-assault-victim).   Criminals and predators may or may not be other students. They could just happen to be in the same bar you're in and you could find yourself in the wrong place at the wrong time.

The bottom line is that problems can potentially exist on *any* campus, in *any* town, in *any* country. With the increased use of the Internet and social media, problems now aren't just isolated locally—they can go national or global in the blink of an eye. Just because it hasn't happened before, or hasn't happened in a long time, does not mean that threats to your personal safety and well-being do not exist. They do, and the sooner you understand that, the better off, and the safer, you will be. In addition to the threats mentioned above from others, there is another group of threats to your personal safety, and that is those from Mother Nature.

No matter where you live, work or go to school, the potential exists for nature to give you problems. The following is a partial list designed to get you thinking about threats to your personal safety that you may not have considered before.

- Is your college near a river that is prone to flooding? Having an escape route away from flooded roadways should be considered.
- Do train tracks or major highways pass by your campus? If so, the possibility of chemical and hazardous waste spills could affect where you attend school and force a quick evacuation.
- How about wildfires? Do you go to college in the western part of the US that is prone to them? You need to know beforehand.
- Are you going to school in tornado alley? If you do, you better know how you can stay safe in the event of a tornado touching down near your college, dorm or apartment.
- What about snowstorms? If you attend college in an area prone to large snowfalls, this can cause threats to your

personal safety. Slippery conditions from snow and ice can cause you to fall and hurt yourself. Massive snow loads on buildings can cause them to collapse. Of course, traveling during snow or ice storms is especially treacherous.

- Other threats such as wind damage, hail, lightning, and torrential downpours can occur anywhere and pose no less serious a threat to your personal safety.

Finally, there are global concerns that could affect you and may threaten your personal safety. Mass chaos and riots could erupt out of economic turmoil, social unrest or from demonstrations on campus that turn violent.

Other global concerns that can affect not only the U.S., but the entire world could be large-scale damage to the U.S. electrical grid due to either an act of terrorism, or from a large coronal mass ejection (CME) or solar flare. Even a high-altitude nuclear detonation by a rogue nation over U.S. soil could cause an electro-magnetic pulse (EMP) that would damage our electrical grid in permanent ways. Massive damage to the grid would essentially throw any affected areas back 150 years.

Be smart, be aware and be informed. But most of all, be prepared.

Knowing what can occur near you or to you is the first step. Preparing for that contingency is the next. Practicing what you would do if that were to occur is the third. I'm not trying to scare you, just increase your awareness, but more on that in the next section.

There are two famous sayings that I want you to know:

"Prepare for the worst, and hope for the best." by Benjamin Disraeli

"By failing to prepare, you are preparing to fail." by Benjamin Franklin

These quotes exemplify personal safety but should also be adages to live by because they apply to so many other things—both in college and in life.

Life is full of surprises, but we don't have to be helpless when the unexpected happens. It is a matter of when, not if, that life will decide to throw you a curve ball. You must be prepared for when that occurs because your life may very well depend on it.

Question Series #1: What are your specific concerns? What are you most worried about? Write down the answers to these questions. There are probably some you haven't thought about such as a few of the scenarios I have outlined above. Consult with your local emergency management agency and the *American Red Cross* about the likelihood of different emergencies that could occur in your local area or the areas you travel to frequently. Check out Chapter 8 for travel safety information. Voice your concerns and discuss them with your family and friends. The more support you have, the better it will be for everyone. Don't try to do it all on your own!

Remember—you're all in this together!

Part 2: Armed with Awareness

As I mentioned in Part 1, you must know what the potential threats to your personal safety are in order to be prepared. Defining those threats by educating yourself is the first step, and here is where awareness comes in.

One of the best ways to avoid a bad situation is simple awareness. *Being aware at all times of your environment, your surroundings and those nearby can go a long way toward avoiding a problem or confrontation.*

What is the landscape like around you—flat or hilly? Are you moving through a well-lit and highly populated area or are you on a dimly lit street with few, if any people around? Stick to well-lit, populated areas when traveling and avoid alleys, dark streets, etc.

Notice people and what they are doing, how they are acting, how they are dressed, etc. If other people are near you, are they "hanging out" and standing around, or do they look like they are moving along with a purpose? Don't have your face buried in your cell phone checking texts as you walk between classes, back to your dorm, or heading to your car in a dimly lit parking lot leaving school at night! Be aware! All too often people in general walk with their phone getting most of their attention. This is a BIG problem! Do not be the person that is robbed or worse because you didn't see or hear something that you should have.

If you must check your phone, look around frequently—in front, behind, above, below and side-to-side. Someone could be watching you from a distance and waiting to see just how distracted you are before they make their move. Simply looking up and around will allow you to see things before it is too late. It will also show a potential criminal that you are not someone who they can easily sneak up on. You do not want to be easily surprised! Look confident and know where you are going. Look at others nearby and let them see that you are aware of them—don't stare, but make sure they know you see them. This reduces your attraction to them as a target and may be what causes them to pass you up for easier "prey." If you do feel that you are being followed, or wish to avoid an individual or group in front of you, there are some options. You can cross the street, or turn around and walk briskly around the area. Go into a store, restaurant or other populated area until the perceived threat is gone.

If you notice a person wearing a long trench coat on a 90 degree hot summer day, that should be something you would notice as being out of the ordinary. Seeing someone who appears nervous, looking constantly from side-to-side, continuously patting a pocket to make sure "something" is there, should deserve additional attention. Again, simply being aware of what is going on around you and who is around you can help you be prepared in case your suspicions are justified! If something looks "out of place" be sure to give it additional attention. Don't ignore it as just being "weird!" Ask yourself what you would do if your suspicion turns out to be true! *Have the answer before you need it* and you will greatly reduce your reaction time should something bad happen.

Remember the A.L.E.R.T. acronym when viewing a suspicious person:

A—Alone and appearing nervous
L—Loose and bulky clothing that doesn't fit with the current weather
E—Exposed items like wires that could be connected to explosives
R—Rigid mid-section due to wearing an explosive belt or gun harness
T—Tight hands that could be holding on to a detonation device

Most of us have been told that "If you see something, say something." There is a reason for this. It is designed to make us more aware of what is happening <u>around</u> us so that something bad doesn't happen <u>to</u> us.

We are all caught up in our busy lives, distracted by electronic devices of every size and shape designed to make us more productive, more in-touch and more informed. *The problem is that they desensitize us to our surroundings.* This means that we may fail to notice a potential problem or not see someone near us acting strange and inching closer and closer. You better notice before it is too late!

Looking at your bright phone screen at night can be an even bigger problem. The light from the screen causes your pupils to contract and affects your night vision. This can be a huge problem because if you can't see what is around you at night, it will be that much easier for someone to get close to you before you realize it. Turn your screen brightness down or enable the blue light filter so your night vision is affected as little as possible. Look up frequently and let your eyes adjust to the dark. Scope out where you are walking to before you get there. This is something you should be doing day or night!

When walking, the safest way to walk is towards traffic; it will be that much harder for someone to stop a vehicle and attempt to rob you or worse. Stay away from any areas that you cannot see clearly such as landscaping, doorways, and alleyways. Traveling in groups will also be safer than traveling alone and you will be less likely to become a victim.

It is also important to keep your hands free so that you can more easily move around and escape. When you are walking towards your vehicle or your door, be sure to have your keys out and ready. If you see any suspicious people either near your car or door, do not continue towards your destination, but instead head to a public location.

We are becoming so dependent on our technology for everything that we are losing touch with our human side that is perceptive and notices the little things. Don't allow yourself to get complacent and oblivious to what is going on around you—both in your immediate vicinity as well as on the world stage. *It is your duty and your responsibility to stay informed.*

Know what events are taking place around the globe that could impact how you live your life. These events could be social, environmental, political or economic, to name just a few. *Do not become so immersed in what you are doing in your daily life that you stop paying attention to what is going on around you—both at home and around the world.*

Many times we feel that unless we have to deal with it *right now*, we can't be bothered. I'm here to tell you that you need to be aware of what is going on around you. This pertains to your town, your state, your country and the world. If you are not, you will be caught unaware, and by then it will be too late to do anything about it.

Don't be stuck unprepared and unaware. Remember, if you are "armed with awareness™," it is something that cannot be taken away from you. Awareness is with you all the time and can serve you well in the days, weeks, months and years ahead. Make it a habit to always operate in a state of heightened awareness and increase your awareness based on risk factors. You should be more aware at night, when alone or while traveling in unfamiliar areas to name a few places where heightened awareness should be practiced.

Chapter 1 Checklist: Your Safety Concerns

✓ Everyone has specific concerns regarding their personal safety. On this page, enter those concerns so that you more readily identify them. This list will change over time. Track them and be sure to review and edit them as necessary. They are broken into organized sections.

Personal Safety Concerns:

Party Safety Concerns:

Online Safety Concerns:

Financial Safety Concerns:

Peer / Boyfriend / Girlfriend Concerns:

Environmental Safety Concerns:

Local Safety Concerns:

Global Safety Concerns:

Other Safety Concerns:

✓ <u>Be Armed With Awareness!</u> One of the best ways to avoid a bad situation is simple awareness. *Being aware at all times of your environment, your surroundings and those nearby can go a long way toward avoiding a problem or confrontation.*

✓ <u>Remember the A.L.E.R.T. acronym when viewing a suspicious person:</u>

A—Alone and appearing nervous
L—Loose and bulky clothing that doesn't fit with the current weather
E—Exposed items like wires that could be connected to explosives
R—Rigid mid-section due to wearing an explosive belt or gun harness
T—Tight hands that could be holding onto a detonation device

CHAPTER 2

Personal Safety Guidelines

Part 1: Establishing Personal Boundaries

Everyone has a different point at which they decide enough is enough. This personal breaking point exists for each situation that pushes us to our limits of tolerance. It can occur when we are being harassed, embarrassed, made fun of, mentally tormented, physically abused, etc.

Our personal space is also an area where we have boundaries. If someone gets too close to you or in your face, you must have a predetermined and established "line" that will force you to act if crossed. This can be a physical line such as when someone gets too close, or it can be an invisible mental or emotional "line in the sand." The important thing for each one of us is to recognize what it is and when someone crosses it.

Your physical personal space includes an area around you that extends out from your body a certain distance depending upon various factors. Things such as whether or not you know the other person, if they are of the same gender or opposite gender, and relationship status are considered. It will also be different for professional, personal and romantic relationships. Another consideration to be made is when traveling to other countries. Some countries may have differently defined comfortable personal space distances than your home country. Research this before traveling.

According to TheSpruce.com in their "Etiquette Rules of Defining Personal Space" article (https://www.thespruce.com/etiquette-rules-of-defining-personal-space-1216625), and according to

Ralph Adolphs, professor of psychology and neuroscience at the California Institute of Technology, in an article (http://www .livescience.com/20801-personal-space.html) on LiveScience.com, the average comfort levels of personal space in the U.S. are:

- 0 to 18 inches for intimate relationships
- 1.5 to 3 feet for good friends and family members
- 3 to 10 feet for casual acquaintances and co-workers
- 4 feet or more for strangers
- 12 feet or more when speaking or addressing a large group

Some general rules of personal space are:

- never touch someone you do not know
- do not reach for or touch someone's child (unless you are being asked to hold a baby or for some other valid reason)
- stand at least four feet away from people in most situations
- if someone leans away or moves away, you are most likely invading that person's space and they are uncomfortable
- do not look through another person's belongings
- refrain from touching anyone unless you know them very well including slapping them on the back, hugging them, playfully punching them, etc.
- be cognizant of personal space when driving by not tailgating
- always knock before entering a room or office
- maintain professionalism and space in your work environment
- don't cut in front of other people in line

Anything that comes inside the area you define may be perceived as a threat to your personal safety. If someone does invade your personal space and make you uncomfortable, you can deal with it in several ways depending upon the situation and the person.

First, you can accept it, uncomfortable as it may be. You also may not be able to move if you are seated at a desk, for example. The other person may simply not be aware of what they are doing. If they are not perceived as a threat, this is one option. If you are able to move away, this is another option. Either lean away from them or step away and hope that the other person takes the hint. You can also come right out and tell the other person that you are uncomfortable with how close they are and ask them to move away. You can explain that you need more space and are not comfortable with how close they are to you.

So why is this important? Well for starters, it will help you deal with others on both a personal and professional level by hopefully addressing the situation up front before things get worse. If you don't know your own boundaries, how can you possibly articulate them to someone else?

On the personal side, you may have to deal with people in your life that make you uncomfortable. This can include neighbors, friends, boyfriends/girlfriends, classmates and others in your social circle. Knowing your limits will allow you to tell others whether or not something is acceptable to you. It also enables you to hopefully diffuse a situation before it escalates from a verbal altercation to a physical one.

On the physical side, if someone invades your defined personal space and actually touches you, you must have a response. They could be poking, pushing, hitting or touching you inappropriately. Whatever the case may be, an <u>immediate and decisive response</u> is necessary in order to assert your feelings over their unwanted contact.

The first thing to do if your personal space is intruded upon is to stay calm. Follow the advice given above first. Lashing out immediately should not be your first course of action unless the threat of bodily harm is imminent. Instead, keep your eyes on the person and your hands in front of you—ready to act if necessary. Do you perceive them to be a threat? Look at the other person's body language. Are they standing still? Rocking from side to side? Are they visibly agitated? You must gauge their threat level as quickly and accurately as you can in a very short period of time. If they appear to be a visible, imminent threat to your personal safety, you will respond differently than if they do not. Keep in mind that appearances can be deceiving, so always be on your guard no matter what is happening. Try not to antagonize them further and do not appear to be threatening toward them since this can escalate the situation.

Next, listen to what they are *really* saying. Are they just words that don't match their physical actions? Do the words even make sense? Are they shouting or screaming? Are they making any demands of you or in general? Does what they are agitated about have any credence, that is, are they right? People who know they are right about something will obviously try to convince others that they are. Finally, listen to their voice itself, not what they are saying. Is the pitch of their voice rising? Are they getting louder and louder? Are the words coming out faster and faster? These are all signs that something worse could be imminent. Be on high alert and try to distance yourself from them by slowly moving away from them. Do not take your eyes off them for even a second.

It is imperative not to show any fear, even if you are terrified. Do not give in to what they are saying and don't provoke them further if at all possible. Agree with what they are saying—even if you really don't. You are trying to diffuse a potentially dangerous situation, so be careful with the words you use and the tone of your voice. Speak slowly and confidently and maintain good posture as you address the person. Let them know both verbally and visually that you are not intimidated.

As you address the person, use simple language and be clear in what you want them to do or stop doing. Attempt to bridge the gap by using the "Feel→Felt" line of communication by saying something like "I understand why you would *feel* this way, I have *felt* that way in the past, but what I really need is . . ." This helps establish some common ground that may help you convince or reason with the person. Finish that statement with a confident, commanding statement of what you want them specifically to do, such as ". . . for you to _____." This fill-in-the-blank can include something like "let me get around you" or "allow me to get back to work" or "to step aside and let me pass."

The majority of the time these things will diffuse the situation. However, there may be a time when no matter what you do works. You must be prepared mentally and physically for that potential outcome and be ready to act accordingly. Physical violence is sometimes the only thing that is going to happen because it is inevitable. The person has already made up their mind and there is nothing that you can say or do that will change that.

If there are other people around, responding in a progressively LOUDER voice will draw attention to the situation and hopefully bring others over to see what is going on. Using short, strong commands like "STOP" or "GET OUT" will be most effective when used in conjunction with the appropriate body language like holding up a hand or pointing. *You are trying to get your point across clearly and in such a way that it cannot be misunderstood.* Always keep in mind that things may escalate rapidly, so be prepared for that contingency.

Remember that if something doesn't seem right or feel right, you should listen to your gut. Intuition can be a powerful ally, especially during a rapidly escalating situation. If the hair on the back of your neck is standing up, your heart is racing, and a really bad feeling comes over you, do not ignore it! It is your intuition telling you something, so you better listen to it and be ready to act without hesitation on the course of action you plan on. Whether you choose to run or fight, be decisive!

Part 2: Routines, Comfort Zones and Statistics

You have a right to be safe, secure and comfortable. How do you feel right now? Do you feel safe? If so, why? Chances are if you are in a familiar environment, you equate that with being safe. The unknown is what makes us uneasy and can make us feel uncomfortable.

During the course of your day, you engage in a pattern of behavior that revolves in large part around your daily routine. At home, you know every inch of your room that you have slept in countless times. This familiarity is comforting and is a "comfort zone" for you. You know your neighborhood and most likely your neighbors. You are used to shopping at the same supermarket, go to the same place to get your hair cut, and walk your dog along the same streets day after day.

The routines we all follow are the things in our lives that give us comfort. People, places and things that are around us on a daily basis are familiar to us. Remove those things, and our anxiety levels shoot up! If you woke up tomorrow in a room you didn't recognize in a town you didn't know surrounded by strangers, how would you feel? I'm guessing pretty unsafe! The reason for this isn't necessarily that you are in danger, but your familiar surroundings have been replaced by things that are foreign to you. This causes you to be very uncomfortable and probably a bit freaked out! This is normal, and it would happen to anyone in the same situation.

Now think about your safety in other places. When you go to the bank, do you feel safe because of the armed guard at the door? On a college campus, does the presence of campus security guards give you a sense of safety? Of course it does! Be extra vigilant when going to public places such as laundromats and public restrooms. The same holds true when using public transportation such as buses and subways. You must ratchet up your awareness and "safety sense." Using elevators and stairwells in large buildings can be a safety risk as well. Be careful and stay safe!

Statistics show a startling upward trend in violent crimes of all types. Here are some of the raw numbers as compiled by the FBI's Universal Crime Reporting web site related to violent crime (https://ucr.fbi.gov/). Violent crime is defined as crimes of murder, rape, robbery and aggravated assault. The following information comes from this site.

In 2015, the latest year for which data was available when this book was written, there were almost 1.2 million violent crimes nationwide—an increase of close to 4% over 2014. This equates to approximately 373 violent crimes per 100,000 people. Of the total number of violent crimes, aggravated assaults accounted for 63.8%, robberies were 27.3%, rape made up 7.5%, and murder the remaining 1.3%.

Many violent crimes are committed using weapons. Firearms were used in 71.5% of murders, 40.8% of robberies, and 24.2% of aggravated assaults. The statistics for rape were not collected.

Specifically related to colleges and universities, this site has the following data compiled for 2014—the most recent available.

Out of a nationwide subset representing 8.3 million college students in 679 universities and campuses in the United States, there were 3,331 violent crimes reported. Those violent crimes as defined above were made up of 13 murders, 1,294 rapes, 654 robberies, and 1,370 aggravated assaults.

Property crimes made up another 69,502 consisting of 5,847 burglaries, 1,822 vehicle thefts, 209 counts of arson, and the remaining 61,833 were larceny (non-violent) thefts.

When you put actual numbers and statistics to the problem, you begin to understand that the problem of violent crime, both nationwide and on college campuses, is real. *It should not and cannot be ignored.* Thinking it won't happen to you is the single biggest mistake you can make.

I encourage you to visit the above-referenced web site and build a custom query for your state or for any colleges you may be considering attending. What you find may surprise you. Educate yourself using this book and other reference materials to understand further the scope of the issue. Talk to your parents and friends about your concerns (as defined in the first chapter). Being aware that a problem exists is the first step toward finding a solution. Ignoring it and wishing it would go away does nothing to help keep you safer when you are at college and on or around campus.

Part 3: Dealing with a "Problem" Roommate

Much as you would like to believe that you will get along with everyone, there is a chance that you may end up with a roommate that you don't always get along with. The college admissions process tries to do the best it can when putting people together. However, there is a very good possibility that it won't always be smooth sailing with your "roomie."

One of the most important things you must do is *communicate effectively* about your needs and expectations. The more roommates, the tougher this is. You must learn to coexist peacefully and be willing to compromise and agree on things that are important to you. It could be study times, sleep times, having guests over, cooking habits, cleanliness (or lack of it) and many others. Living with another person (or persons) can be very stressful and challenging for everyone involved, but a valuable experience.

As a freshman, you will be dealing with a roommate (or two or three). In subsequent years, you may have different roommates and perhaps even an apartment off-campus. You need to learn to live with people who have different priorities and ways of doing things. Compromise is the name of the game, so learn this "lesson" well!

Having expectations of the other person, and living up to their expectations of you is essential to living harmoniously. Do your part, because there are going to be habits or traits that annoy your roommate and drive them crazy about you! Yes, we all have our faults. Living with someone else is one of the fastest ways to learn what they are! Be prepared to get some constructive criticism and take it without getting offended. This can be a very good learning experience for you and gives you a chance to see how others view you along with all your faults.

When you have a problem with your roommate, talk to them. Don't get angry, rude or belligerent about it. Politely discuss what is bothering you like an adult; chances are your roommate has no idea what they are doing is making you nuts! Most reasonable people will be willing to come to some sort of compromise or agreement. Once you do, you will be able to live together free of tension. It will only get worse if you don't.

One thing to be aware of—don't get caught up in every little thing that you don't like about your roommate. Instead, focus on the BIG deal items that you cannot live with. Everyone has small quirks and habits that may annoy other people. Decide whether or not the "problem" is worth stressing over. If you can find a way to deal with it, great. If not, prioritize it. Start with the major issues and go from there.

If you are still having trouble with your roommate after trying to do all that you can and not getting anywhere, it may be time to talk to your Resident Assistant (RA). They are available to help in a variety of ways and may have some ideas. If possible, they can help you facilitate a truce or understanding with your "problem" roommate so that you can coexist and not drive each other crazy. RAs want their floor or building to be a positive experience for the residents who live there.

They care about your well-being and are there to help, so let them! If you simply cannot get along, you may have to move rooms.

Chapter 2 Checklist: Personal Boundaries

✓ Personal boundaries govern your comfort zone. Only you know what makes you feel uncomfortable and when you have been pushed to your breaking point. This point exists for each person, but everyone is different. <u>Know your limits and clearly define them in this section.</u>

Emotional Limits: *(example: someone who takes advantage of your forgiving nature to continually treat you badly)*

_____

Mental Limits: *(example: someone continually tells lies regarding your intelligence in front of one of your professors)*

_____

Physical Limits: *(example: someone screams at you 2" from your nose, or perhaps grabs you inappropriately)*

_____

Identify places that you frequent as part of your routine that could become dangerous due to complacency unless you are continually vigilant. _____

✓ Don't think "it" can't happen to you—it can and it will! Have the foresight to recognize when you are entering an area that could present a hazard to your personal safety.

CHAPTER 3

Bullying & Hazing

Part 1: Bullying

Bullying has been around since the beginning of time. Those who were bigger and stronger have always been able to get those who were smaller and weaker to do as they wanted. This is true of all sorts of creatures—insects, animals and of course, people. With regard to people, bullying can include threats, spreading rumors, physical, mental or emotional attacks, and exclusion from group activities among others.

Bullying exists in many forms:

- between two people
- between many people and one person
- between two groups of people
- between towns
- between towns and people
- between businesses
- between businesses and customers
- between governments
- between governments and their citizens
- between countries
- between countries and their citizens

If one entity is stronger than another, it is able to get the weaker of the two to submit or agree to its demands or face the consequences.

Simply put, bullying is one form of repetitive harassment or aggressive behavior that involves a real or perceived power imbalance. It is inflicted by an abuser of greater physical and/or social power and dominance than the victim. Bullying is often done with clear intentions of establishing dominance of the target through different means. These means may include: verbal harassment, physical assault, emotional blackmail, or other more subtle methods of coercion such as manipulation of the victim. Effects can be long-lasting and potentially cause problems for years for the victim.

Bullies are often characterized as having authoritarian personalities. They also feel a strong need to control or dominate anything, be it a weaker person, a stronger person, or a situation. They have also been noted to display deficiency in terms of social skills and possess a prejudice against subordinates. Studies have shown that most bullies have envy and resentment as motives for bullying. Researchers have identified some risk factors. These include quickness to anger, use of force, addiction to aggressive behaviors, mistaking another person's actions as hostile, concern with preserving the self image, and engaging in obsessive actions.

As mentioned above, bullying exists in varied settings of social interaction including schools, workplaces, inside the home, and around the neighborhood. It may occur between different social groups, social classes and even between countries. *Like any kind of abusive behavior, bullying is a repetitive act done to gain power or control over another person, race, or country.*

Bullying is generally classified into two types:

Direct bullying. This type of bullying can take different forms. The bully can display *physical aggression* in the form of shoving, poking, pinching, spitting, tripping, taking or breaking possessions, throwing things, slapping, choking, punching, kicking and beating. There can also be direct *verbal bullying* such as teasing, name-calling, threats of physical harm, inappropriate comments of a sexual nature, making mean, rude or obscene gestures, and taunting.

Indirect bullying. Also called social aggression, the victim is forced into social isolation. This is usually done by badmouthing the victim, spreading false rumors about the victim, refusing to socialize with the victim, name calling, mocking the victim, embarrassing the victim, forcing other people to avoid socializing with the victim and other forms of manipulation. The rapid rise of various social network sites online has enabled this form of bullying (cyber-bullying) to grow at an alarming pace. It has caused victims to commit violent acts toward others or themselves in an effort to escape. More on cyber-bullying is discussed in the next section.

It can also happen in the victim's neighborhood. A 2013 *CDC Youth Risk Behavior Surveillance System* (http://www.cdc.gov/HealthyYouth/yrbs/index.htm) indicates that nationwide, approximately 20% of students in high school (grades 9–12) experience bullying. The *National Center for Education Statistics 2012–13 School Crime Supplement* (http://nces.ed.gov/pubs2015/2015056.pdf) found that 22% of students ages 12–18 experience bullying. These are shockingly high percentages that indicate bullying is a huge problem in schools, with greater than one out of five students being the victim at some point. Cyber-bullying statistics are harder to come by as online social media sites change rapidly, but we will discuss that later on in this book.

Adult Bullying. When we talk or read about bullying, many people assume it's about younger kids doing mean things to each other. It can be the result of a variety of things including immaturity. So why is it that although we don't hear a lot about adult bullying, that it exists—and to quite a large degree?

First of all, adult bullying can be more serious than the sort of bullying that is experienced by children on the schoolyard. It may not be discussed as much or addressed in society the same way, but it exists nonetheless. Adult bullying may even require legal action in some cases.

Adult bullies are more prone to utilize indirect bullying techniques on their victims. Often this happens in the workplace, where managers can bully lower level employees into doing things that are not required of them in their job position. Due to the threat of being reprimanded, written up or fired, they are forced to do things they do not want to do. This is done by the bully who often lacks confidence. They use their position of authority to feel better about themselves by humiliating others and making them do their bidding. *This can actually be criminal depending upon the circumstances in which employees are forced to do things.* Creating a hostile work environment is against the law.

There are several different types of adult bullies; each is unique.

1. Verbally Abusive Adult Bully—As the name implies, these types of bullies use words to inflict humiliation or make demeaning and derogatory comments about their victim. Since it is verbal in nature, it is difficult to prove or document unless there are other witnesses to it. Those who find themselves on the receiving end of verbally abusive bosses can be damaged emotionally and psychologically. This can lead to depression and poor job performance which can ultimately lead to job loss and unemployment for the victim. This downward spiral can be extremely difficult to break out of since the victim feels that they must not be worthy since they were fired or let go. Their confidence is shattered and self-esteem suffers mightily.

2. Physically Abusive Adult Bully—Although bullying by adults tends to be mostly verbal, there are occasions where things can turn physical. It usually begins with the bully making verbal threats of physical harm to the victim, but may escalate to actual physical violence. More than likely some other form of physical abuse occurs such as the physical taking of the victim's property or damage to the victim's property. This can include articles of clothing (think of spilling coffee on a nice white shirt) or office supplies (stealing all the pens out of someone's desk, for example) or any number of things. They could write anonymous notes about the victim, or write notes to other employees and sign the victim's name to them, causing others to think that the victim is to blame rather than the bully.

3. Secondary Adult Bully—An adult may join in the abuse and bullying that is directed toward another person if they know that it will spare them that same abuse. It isn't that they have malicious intent on their own; they are simply worried about saving their own skin. They may even feel

bad about it, but not bad enough to stand up to the person who is initiating the bullying toward the other person.

If you are the victim of bullying in your place of work, the first thing to do is report it to your supervisor. If your immediate supervisor is the one doing the bullying, then go up to their boss or the owner of the company. If the owner of the company is the one who is bullying you, it may be time to seek legal counsel or look for another job.

You can possibly report the person or company to various organizations such as *OSHA*, the *US Department of Labor* or the *US Equal Employment Opportunity Commission*, but you need to have proof and documentation of what is occurring. There are many laws and acts that protect workers including *The Fair Labor Standards Act*, *The National Labor Relations Act*, *The Family and Medical Leave Act*, *Americans With Disabilities Act* and others. Without proof, your options are limited. Review your company's policies and procedures as well as any internal memos or regulations that address bullying in the workplace. If there aren't any, ask your supervisor (unless they are the bully) to put some in place to protect the employees and let them know why. You can also reference the above acts and laws that apply to your situation; they exist to protect you! Be sure to document all instances of workplace bullying and note the date, the time, anyone else who is present who could be a witness, and as much detail as possible about the incident(s). This documentation can be of great help if things escalate to a legal battle.

You may choose to simply ignore the bully and not let them get to you. If the bullying is by a co-worker and no one else is around to witness these events, try not to let them bother you. Know that you do have options. Remember that bullying is not a legitimate form of management and it is inappropriate to bully co-workers or those you manage. It also decreases employee productivity and increases employee turnover. Some specific examples of college student, adult and workplace bullying include:

- repeated harassment or humiliating actions
- shouting, threatening or screaming

- sabotaging the work of others
- constantly criticizing and constant negative feedback
- setting impossible deadlines or tasks to perform
- taking credit for the work of another person
- spreading false rumors
- assigning trivial or menial work that is demeaning

As a result of bullying, the victim may find they are affected psychologically and physically depending on the severity of the bullying that they are experiencing. Increased pressure and stress can lead to trouble sleeping and a feeling of dread as the time approaches to go to work or school. Often low self-esteem and depression can be experienced as feelings of shame and guilt begin to affect the person.

These can in turn lead to very real physical ailments related to the increase in stress such as headaches, insomnia, reduced overall health and lowered immune system response. These all can lead to a further decline in health. Problems with digestion and high blood pressure can also affect the person. In fact, PTSD (post-traumatic stress disorder) can be brought on as an eventual problem due to all the negative factors being experienced.

Want to throw the bully off-guard? Agree with them! They won't know what to say next because they will expect you to argue with them. This might diffuse the situation immediately and leave them speechless!

So why do bullies act this way? Studies have shown some bullies do it to be thought of as popular or tough, or sometimes just to get attention. Bullies are said to also do it out of jealousy, or they may simply be acting out because they were bullied earlier in their own lives. Some bullies come from abusive families and neighborhoods. Whatever the cause, it is never fun when facing a bully or group of bullies.

Being subject to bullying often may contribute to developing an inferiority complex. This is a feeling of being inferior to others in one way or another. Constantly being mocked or criticized in a negative way by bullies may force a person to start believing those lies and lose faith in themselves. Victims may also be more prone to developing stress-related

mental conditions such as anxiety and depression from frequent bullying.

*Victims should know that they are not the problem, the bul-
lies are.* Victims should <u>not</u> start second-guessing themselves
just because bullies tell them they're no good. *Being different
shouldn't rob you of your right to personal security.* Don't be
ashamed of your differences, be proud of them. It's not your
fault you are unique—we all are!

A good way to avoid being bullied is to go out with a group,
making it difficult for bullies to single you out. If this doesn't
work, it would help to tell someone you trust that someone is
bullying you. Having someone mediate for you does not make
you a coward. Remember, *keeping yourself safe should matter
more than what others think.*

<u>Boosting your confidence can do wonders for warding off
bullies</u>. If a bully senses any fear or nervousness on the part
of the victim, they will be quick to pounce! However, if you
exude confidence and show that you are unaffected, chances
are they will move onto another less confident victim who will
make an easier target. *Most bullies do not like conflict and will
try to avoid it at all possible because it represents a challenge
to their ability to bully!*

With regard to facing multiple bullies, there are three essential rules:

1. Remember, most of those in the group probably are fol-
   lowers who lack confidence. Stand up to the "leader" and
   watch the rest hesitate or scatter.
2. During the confrontation, you only want to face a single
   bully at one time. If you get caught between two or more
   bullies you can be surprised or "sucker punched." Try to
   determine the leader of the group or who appears to be the
   most immediate threat and deal with them first.
3. Always try to keep one bully between you and the other
   bullies! This will allow you to only face one at a time,
   enabling you to deal with them one at a time if necessary.

If you follow these rules, you stand a much better chance of
overcoming the ordeal since you are putting yourself in a position

to only have to deal with one attacker or bully at a time. *This is also the secret to surviving an attack by multiple assailants.*

If you are being bullied there are several specific steps you can take.

Reach Out

If your campus has a *Public Safety* or *Security Department*, let them know what is occurring. Most departments offer escorts if you ask for one. Sometimes you may have to tell more than one person before you get results. Ask your friends to help you. Remember, there is safety in numbers. It is also a good idea to practice what to say the next time you're bullied with your parents, teachers or friends.

Be Cool in the Moment

Stay calm and confident. Don't show the bully that they are getting to you or in your head. Try not to show that you're sad or mad, but ignore the bully and walk away. Remember that fighting can make bullying worse, so only do so as a last resort. If it comes to that, take out the leader first without hesitation and watch the rest hesitate and lose confidence.

School and Community Action

It is important to work with others to stop bullying. When bullying is reduced or eliminated, the entire school and every student benefits. Many people of all ages cope with bullying; you are not alone. No one deserves to be bullied and you must take action if it happens to you.

Now, you may not be the person being bullied, but you may witness bullying happening to someone else. Don't ignore it! There are many things you can do to help.

-Interrupt the bully by trying to change the subject or redirect their attention away from the person being bullied.

-You can speak up for the person being bullied in a positive way.

-You can simply ask the bully to stop; they may or may not, but ask!

-The person being bullied needs comfort and understanding; offer it.

-If you are not comfortable confronting the bully on your own, you can walk away and get help by finding an adult or others to intervene.

If you are the bully . . .

First of all, *you* can decide to change.

No one is forcing you to be a bully. Perhaps there are some underlying problems that are causing you to act out in this way. You may or may not realize why or that what you are doing is considered bullying. Recognize your behavior and make a conscious decision to change.

It will help if you talk to someone about it. It can be an adult such as a parent or teacher about how you can change in order to to get along better with other people.

You can ask a friend to help you recognize and stop your bullying behavior. Once you learn to recognize this behavior as it is occurring, you can stop doing it. A great first step toward changing your attitude and negative behavior is to apologize to the people you have bullied in the past. Let them know that you understand it was hurtful and you didn't realize how your behavior and bullying toward them was having an impact.

Be Personally Responsible

One of the best ways to begin to understand what it is like to be bullied is to think about what it feels like. It is obviously not a positive experience. In fact, it can be a very hurtful and damaging experience on many levels—emotional, mental and even physical. Ask yourself if you would want to be treated in the same manner. The answer is an obvious and emphatic "No!" If you don't want someone else treating *you* this way, then why in the world are you treating someone else that way? The answer is, you shouldn't!

Finally, before you say a word to someone else that could be construed as negative or bullying in nature, listen to how it sounds in your own mind. If it is negative and could be hurtful to another person, then don't say it! Either say nothing, or rephrase what you are trying to say in a more positive, or at the very least, a neutral way.

Change Your Behavior

Let's be real; if you don't *want* to change, you won't. It doesn't matter if we're talking about bullying, quitting smoking, eating healthy or any one of many other negative and/or destructive habits that people have.

Hopefully those who are reading this don't engage in bullying (or any negative) behavior. But again, that's not realistic. We *all* have things we would like to change about ourselves. It could be our level of fitness, our eating habits, our study habits, our dating habits or our work ethic.

There is a proven method that can help you break any bad habit in less than a month. Don't believe me? Then prove me wrong and try it! What have you got to lose, other than a bad habit? Read on to learn how . . .

It is possible for anyone to break a bad habit, change their behavior, or form a new habit within about 30 days. How is this possible?

First, identify the behavior or habit that you wish to break or establish. As an example, let's use a typical bad habit that many college students have—procrastination!

Second, speak out loud the habit you wish to break *as if you already do not do it.* (If you are trying to establish a good habit, speak about it as if you already do it.)

Third, say the statement *out loud* twice a day—once when you wake up in the morning, and once before you go to bed. You could tape it to your bathroom mirror so you won't forget, since that is typically where most people start and end their day. Do this for 30 days and be amazed!

For our example, we will create the following statement: "I am someone who gets my work and studying done early." Notice the lack of the words "don't" or "do not." The reason is that you only want to use positive words in your "habit-breaking" or "habit-forming" phrase. *This will not work if you use negative words because negative words are not accepted by your subconscious, therefore you cannot use them in your statement.*

What you are basically doing with this exercise is literally programming your subconscious to form this new habit. In order to do so, you simply use positive reinforcement. The statement "I will not put off doing my assignments until the last minute" is actually worse! You are reinforcing putting off your assignments until the last minute because your subconscious cannot ignore the words "will not" from the statement. Make sense? Try it, and within 30 days you will form a new habit, or break a bad one!

Now to break the bad habit specifically in terms of being a bully, start off by resisting any pressure from your peers to bully others. Many bullies feel empowered when they have the support of others. Take away that support, and they feel less likely to follow through with their plans if they know that others won't follow along and support them.

Step one is that if you start to bully someone, or if you are around others who are, simply walk away and find something else to do. Now, as mentioned above, this doesn't help the person being bullied. However, in the beginning stages of your transition from "bully" to "supporter of the bullied," it may be easier to just distance yourself as quickly as possible.

Step two is to begin to hear what you really say to others. You may not realize how hurtful your tone or the actual words you are saying can be. Try talking out loud to yourself when you are alone, or record yourself and then listen to the recording. This way you get to hear what you actually sound like. It may surprise you and be a wake up call that really gets you to understand how tone and delivery can be just as negative as the actual words you say.

The bottom line is that you don't have to like everyone around you, but you do have to treat everyone with respect! If you don't respect other people, then they will not respect you—it's as simple as that. Get on the right path now and watch how things change for the better in your relationships with everyone in your life.

Part 2: Hazing

A form of bullying that is commonly found in fraternities and sororities is hazing. Hazing encompasses ceremonies, abuse and humiliation that are used as a way to initiate a person into a group, team or club.

Hazing is typically harmless and used as a rite of passage into an organization. However, in recent years, it has become increasingly dangerous, particularly in larger colleges and universities. The most benign results of hazing are usually embarrassment and being pressured to do things in order to be accepted. It can involve deception in order to test one's loyalty to the group. One example is being blindfolded and tricked into walking over "glass" that is really only potato chips. Those being initiated prove they are loyal by completing the tasks that are assigned without question. These types of hazing activities are relatively harmless. Having to eat disgusting foods or drink foul-tasting liquids are also common during hazing rites.

Drinking games or having to drink certain amounts of alcohol in specified periods of time can be very dangerous. This fatal outcome befell a student in early 2017 at a pledge party. As a result, some fraternity brothers were charged, and may even up in jail as a result. The case is one of the largest hazing prosecutions in history.

Unfortunately, the incident is not an isolated one. A student who died from an unexplained illness earlier that same year is believed to have been forced to drink a toxic substance. It put him in the hospital for days and he ended up losing his life.

Hazing can be relatively harmless, but as these two examples illustrate, it can turn deadly. Most colleges and universities have an anti-hazing policy, but simply having a policy does not prevent it from occurring. If you are pledging, do not feel like you must do something that could jeopardize your personal safety. It is simply not worth the risk!

Anti-Bullying Tips

Anti-Bullying Tip #1: Be an *upstander*, not a *bystander*.

Bystanders simply watch, walk by or ignore a situation. Don't be someone who does nothing. Instead be an "upstander" and stand up for the person being bullied. What does an upstanding person do? *The right thing at the appropriate time.*

This is an excellent way to turn conventional thinking about not wanting to get involved around. When we stand up for someone else, it gives that person confidence. It lets them know that other people care enough about them to "stand up" for them. This simple act can do wonders for those with low self-esteem, which may be part of the reason why they were being bullied in the first place. Lack of confidence is a huge reason why many people are targeted by bullies. They are easy, soft targets who have low self-esteem and lack confidence in themselves.

Anti-Bullying Tip #2: *Have courage* to do the right thing and don't worry about what other people will think or say about you.

When you witness another person being bullied, it is easy to simply turn and walk in the opposite direction and not get involved. Most people fall into this category—they simply do not want to get involved. Humans by nature do not like conflict.

Unfortunately, if more people were brave enough and had the courage to interrupt a bully, the problem would not be nearly as big. With the growth of social media, the rise of cyber-bullying has even wider and greater implications, but more on that topic later.

Anti-Bullying Tip #3: Think about the victim and those around you.

We all want to be treated with respect, and everyone deserves to be treated equally. When you stand up for someone else, it sends a message to others that this kind of treatment is not okay around you. This will elevate your status among your peers as someone who is not afraid to do the right thing. You do it whether or not you know the person and regardless of what others may think. It also increases their respect for you.

Anti-Bullying Tip #4: Think about how you would feel if someone came to your defense and gave you their support.

If a total stranger came to your aid, how would that make you feel? I think it's safe to say that it would make you feel pretty awesome! To have someone help you who didn't need to, yet went out of their way to assist is indeed a very special thing.

Unfortunately, it doesn't happen enough today because most people simply do not want to get involved in things that don't concern them. What they don't realize is that it makes society a much better place when people look out for each other.

Anti-Bullying Tip #5: You have an ethical right and a moral obligation to help others.

Bullies have no right to harass, intimidate or hurt another person. However, you do have the right to stop the bullying behavior from continuing! Every single person has a set of morals that they live by. If we see something that goes against our morals, it troubles us. This includes seeing someone being bullied. Most people would say that it is morally wrong and should not be allowed to continue.

You have the right to step in and stop bullying MORE than a bully has the right to intimidate, hurt and scare another person.

Anti-Bullying Tip #6: Don't ignore the situation, but don't put yourself in harm's way either.

Bullying can occur on a variety of levels—from the relatively benign to the downright dangerous. If you feel that the situation is getting out of hand or you are too uncomfortable, then don't! But do get additional help as soon as possible!

Don't make the mistake of trying to help someone when the numbers are greatly to your disadvantage. Get others to assist such as adults, teachers, friends or even the police if the situation is getting bad enough. It is not worth putting your own life and well-being at risk to help someone else. You may have the best intentions, but also be realistic.

If you witness someone being physically harassed by five people who appear to be violent, crazy or both, I do not recommend putting your own personal safety at risk to step in and help! Go get help in one form or another. If you make a call or text people to come assist you, stay in the area and keep an eye on things until help arrives—hopefully before anything too bad happens. Remember, it will do you no good if you are also caught up in a violent altercation. What good is it if there are two victims instead of just one! Again, if it feels like you can't handle it on your own, do not hesitate to get additional help.

Anti-Bullying Tip #7: If it feels wrong, it probably is.

The phrase "trust your gut" means that you intuitively know whether or not something is right or wrong. If you get the feeling that something just isn't right, it probably isn't. Assess what is going on to the best of your ability and then act accordingly by either stepping in or getting more help.

Anti-Bullying Tip #8: When in doubt, be nice.

Sometimes we find ourselves in a situation that we are unsure of as to the motives of the others around us. It is always prudent to err on the side of caution and try to be amicable. Don't antagonize others who you feel may be volatile. If you have to agree with what they are saying, then do so. If it means diffusing a potentially explosive situation, do what is necessary to keep yourself safe. Maintain a positive attitude and be nice to the others around you. Don't give them a reason to turn on you and have the situation quickly turn bad. Seek to appease them so that you can make a hasty retreat as soon as you are able.

Chapter 3 Checklist: Bullying

✓ Bullying can include threats, spreading rumors, physical, mental or emotional attacks, and exclusion from group activities. It exists in many forms including between people, organizations, companies, and countries. If one entity is stronger than another, it is able to get the weaker of the two to submit or agree to its demands or face the consequences.

✓ Bullying is generally classified into 2 types:

1. Direct bullying—this includes *physical aggression* in the form of shoving, poking, pinching, choking, punching, kicking, spitting, tripping, taking or breaking possessions, and throwing things. There can also be direct *verbal bullying* such as teasing, name-calling, threats of physical harm, inappropriate comments of a sexual nature, and making rude or obscene gestures.

2. Indirect bullying—this causes the victim to be forced into social isolation. This is usually done by badmouthing the

victim, spreading false rumors, refusing to socialize with the victim, name calling, mocking, embarrassing the victim, forcing other people to avoid socializing with the victim and other forms of manipulation.

✓ There are several different types of adult bullies:

1. <u>Verbally Abusive Adult Bully</u>—these types of bullies use words to inflict humiliation or make demeaning and derogatory comments about their victim.
2. <u>Physically Abusive Adult Bully</u>—Although bullying by adults tends to be mostly verbal, there are occasions where things can turn physical.
3. <u>Secondary Adult Bully</u>—An adult may join in the abuse and bullying that is directed toward another person if they know that it will spare them that same abuse.

✓ <u>Boosting your confidence can do wonders for warding off bullies</u>. *Most bullies do not like conflict and will try to avoid it at all possible because it represents a challenge to their ability to bully!*

CHAPTER 4

Cyber-Bullying

The meteoric rise of electronic devices connected to the Internet allows us to instantly communicate with people around the world just as easily as with our friends across town. Gadgets of every size and shape include everything from the latest smartphones and tablets to laptops and other computing devices. All of them allow our society and our world to be tied together like never before.

There are many great feats that are possible with this technology that now literally exists at our fingertips. Today's sleek and powerful smartphones make yesterday's computers look ancient, both in form and function. We can simply press a button on our smart phone and ask it anything we need to know. Everything from the current temperature to directions to our favorite vacation spot to the answer to that perplexing calculus problem we can't figure out is available. The power is simply astounding, but as the saying goes, with great power comes great responsibility.

The problem with this technology is that it has enabled a new threat to emerge—*cyber-bullying*. Cyber-bullying occurs when electronic devices such as cellular phones, computers & tablets are used to send text, images, or video that are intended to harass or harm someone. It is similar to off-line bullying, but the difference is that it utilizes the Internet and social media sites. It may also be posted anonymously. This makes it is nearly impossible to control or limit the spread of the offending information once it is online.

Today's technology has also made it possible for an entirely new class of communications applications to arise—social media. These incredible programs allow us to stay in touch with family and friends, and allow us to share information in real time. We can now upload and share pictures and video so that it is instantly viewable online by others.

Facebook, YouTube, Twitter, LinkedIn, Pintrest, Google+, Tumblr, Instagram, SnapChat—the list goes on and on! *Wikipedia* has over 200 different social media sites listed as of this writing, and that list continues to grow. With so many social media outlets for us to communicate on, it is impossible to monitor and determine the content that is posted on all of these sites. However, one disparaging comment posted on just a few of them could end up ruining someone's career or their life.

It is upsetting to read in the news about someone who has been bullied to the point where they decide to either hurt others or take their own life. This is the extreme, but it has happened before, and unfortunately will happen again in the future—all because of bullying or cyber-bullying.

Cyber-bullying is perpetuated by online friends, classmates, ex-boyfriends or ex-girlfriends, and often by anonymous users. Most of the time the victim knows the perpetrator. It may be initiated due to some sort of personal problem that exists between the two. The problem with cyber-bullying is that it doesn't stop there. Once it gets online in whatever form, it is easy to go "viral" and spread all over social media in an extremely short period of time.

This compounds the problem much worse when compared to offline bullying. That would typically be limited to the victim, the bully and perhaps some witnesses. Sure, it might spread around school or town, but that would be it. Nobody in surrounding towns, states or even countries would be aware of it. Today, that is not the case. Information can spread just as easily to any corner of the globe and turn a small problem or conflict into a huge issue. It can even cause legal problems for the person responsible for spreading the malicious information.

There are many types of cyber-bullying. The most obvious is sending bullying or harassing messages directly to someone's cell phone or email account. Since this doesn't involve any other people and isn't posted online, it typically is the easiest to control. This doesn't mean that it is any less damaging to the person who is the victim, but at least it can often be dealt with and isn't all over the Internet.

Another common type of cyber-bullying is making nasty or inappropriate comments about someone on their *Facebook* page or other social networking site. All of that person's "friends" could potentially read those comments and be exposed to them. With literally dozens of popular sites that exist, the task of controlling what is said about a person becomes basically impossible to stop.

A much more embarrassing and potentially damaging type of cyber-bullying involves sending images or video of a sexual, inappropriate or lewd nature to the victim. These could be of the victim, and the bully could threaten to post them online unless the victim does or does not do something. A threat like "You better not tell my boyfriend that I cheated on him or else I'll post this picture of you on *Facebook*!" This form of cyber-bullying is essentially blackmail and you may have legal recourse.

Any sort of messaging system can be utilized to cyber-bully another person. This can involve cell phone texts, instant messaging programs, blogs, email or any number of social media sites. These sites operate as messaging systems including *Twitter*, *SnapChat* and *Instagram* to name a few of the more popular ones.

Instant messaging and social media sites can be used in any number of ways to make another person uncomfortable. This includes anything that is sent or posted such as information about a person's sexual orientation, ethnicity, race, weight, looks, religion, etc. Basically anything that causes someone to feel as if they are inferior or an outcast is valid. This can be a very cruel form of cyber-bullying toward the victim and cause them a great deal of doubt about who they are and what they believe. It can contribute to changes in their demeanor and mental health. They can become depressed, withdrawn and even begin to think about ways to get revenge on those who have made them feel this way. Of course, this can lead to other much more serious problems.

Spreading rumors about another person is a form of bullying that has been around forever. It is done to gain advantage over another person or business, discredit expertise, or simply to get others to think differently. This is true for both people and businesses. Competitors can spread false rumors about their competition in order to increase their own sales and hurt their competition. With the development of social media and the Internet, the spreading of false rumors becomes impossible to control once it starts. Every single thing that is posted or sent online remains there. Even when it is "deleted" it will still exist on backups and on archived versions of web pages. Many people think that when something is deleted it is gone—wrong! It is *never* truly "deleted."

If you don't want to see what you post online showing up on a billboard in Times Square in the middle of New York City, then don't post it! It is akin to doing just that because hundreds, thousands and even millions of people could see it over time. It will always exist somewhere, so think twice before sending because once you press [Send], [Post] or [Tweet], you cannot take it back. The cat is out of the bag!

Creating websites, blogs or social media pages that specifically target another person takes cyber-bullying to the next level. The commitment in time, energy and resources to make this happen is not a trivial one and shows the seriousness of the bully. These sites may contain all sorts of misinformation and gossip, images, videos designed to discredit, embarrass, or make fun of a person, company or product among others.

This sort of behavior may cross the line and be illegal depending on what is posted and who or what it is directed toward. If you experience this type of cyber-bullying, you may have legal recourse to get the information taken down. You would first need to find out where the web site is hosted, and a quick online search will give you that information so that you can proceed with legal action.

There are other forms of illegal cyber-bullying that exist. Using any sort of technology to record another person without their permission is illegal. This includes the use of both audio and video recording devices including cell phones and web cams. If those recordings are then posted online and contain embarrassing or damaging information, the fallout could be massive in terms of its effect on the victim. The legal problems that could exist for the bully may also be significant.

Another illegal form of cyber-bullying is logging into (breaking into) another person's account for the purpose of sending messages or making posts while posing as that person. Not only is this highly illegal, it can be extremely damaging to the person who is "supposedly" the one making the posts, comments, etc. To their friends and others, it appears as if they are actually the ones doing it. There is a certain level of credibility that comes along with that as well. If you appear to post something, and then try to deny it later, you will be hard pressed to prove that it wasn't you. This can cause you to lose friendships, relationships or jobs.

Responding to Immediate Safety Concerns:

As with any form of bullying or harassment, things can go from bad to worse rapidly. Contact your campus security department or call 911 immediately if you feel you are in immediate danger or in fear for your life. *Do not wait and think you are overreacting.* Cyber-bullying is a prosecutable crime, and sometimes even just the threat of legal action can make someone stop.

There are several scenarios that should cause you to contact your campus security department or the police right away. The most obvious is the direct threat of physical harm or death. Do not ignore it, but report it to the authorities *immediately* so that there is a record of it on file. Provide any copies of texts, posts, etc. to law enforcement. They will then have the information to help with their investigation. A threat on your life or a threat of physical harm is a serious thing. Treat it is such and get law enforcement involved right away. If something does happen, there will be a record of what transpired prior and helps to establish motive.

The Internet has also caused a 21st century spin on an age-old crime—stalking. *Cyber-stalking* is another very real and serious crime. It is entirely possible that you can be stalked online and your actions followed. This can of course follow you off-line where it becomes actual physical stalking. If you suspect either of these is occurring, report it to the authorities immediately. It is another area where you want to be sure to establish a record of what is happening to you. Unfortunately, the more it happens, the easier it will be to do something from a legal standpoint such as getting a *Protection From Abuse* order *(PFA)*.

Other forms of more serious cyber-bullying include hate mail. Just as in receiving physical hate mail, you can receive hate email or hate texts, posts, etc. These are serious threats to your personal safety as well, so keep all copies and provide them to law enforcement. Hate mail can be very hurtful, hence its name. Any hate-related communication sent to any of your online accounts should be saved and reported to the authorities. It is no joke and constitutes a direct threat to your safety.

Just as serious, but potentially more embarrassing, are secretly recorded audios or videos of you saying or doing things that you thought were private and then having them become public. Now that they are out there for the whole world to see, they can be very damaging to you both personally and professionally. If they involve you saying something negative about your employer, you may lose your job! The seriousness of this sort of cyber-bullying can be very damaging because there is audio or video evidence of you doing or saying something and this cannot be disputed. There is proof because it is you on the recording.

To protect yourself, be very careful about what you say and do in the "privacy" of your home, dorm room, classroom or place of employment. There are so many video cameras out in the world today that the concept of "privacy" really no longer exists. There are cameras on college campuses, in homes, places of business, city streets, and in many other locations. You need to assume that you are on camera at (almost) all times, and act accordingly. Cameras are obviously inappropriate in certain places such as the bathroom and bedroom.

If you are the victim of cyber-bullying, your first thought may be to retaliate—don't. Remain calm and do not respond based purely on emotions. Responding to the bully demonstrates to them that they are getting to you, and getting a response proves this to them. This could end up causing them to ramp up their efforts once they know they are having an effect. Your best choice is to not engage the bully in any way if at all possible. Instead there are a few proactive things you can do.

First, log into your accounts and block the person or persons who are harassing and bullying you. This includes blocking their phone number from both your cell phone and home phone. Online social media sites such as *Facebook* allow you to easily block people from seeing what you post and from viewing your timeline. They also allow you to report abuse for any offensive content that you receive. It establishes a chain of reporting that shows this is a serious problem. Provide a record to the authorities if you need to prove what is happening to you.

Do the same thing on any other social media sites you are on where the bully or bullies are. Block them, remove them from your address book, etc. You will want to *keep* any correspondence that you have received from them for the authorities as evidence should it come to that. Print out hard copies and begin your own "evidence" folder. This will show any law enforcement or legal professional that you are prepared. It also shows that the problem is serious enough to warrant you taking the measures you have. It will only help to strengthen your case if necessary.

If you see content about you that is offensive in nature appearing on websites, blogs, etc., save and print out hard copies of the material. Put it in your "evidence" folder, and then contact the webmaster or owner of the site to report the person. Request that the information be taken down immediately. You can also let them know that you are the victim and there is a good possibility that any sites displaying offensive or threatening information about you may be involved in a lawsuit. Watch how fast the information comes down! Of course, some sites won't do anything, and that will have to be dealt with down the road. Keep a good record of all these sites because the more evidence you have, the stronger your case will be. Make sure to note the date and time of each post, or the date and time that you first noticed it. Also note the date and time you noticed any information removed from sites. This includes dates and times that you requested people be blocked from various social media sites.

It may sound like a lot of work, but this is your safety and there can be nothing left to chance. If you feel threatened, it is your responsibility to act accordingly to fix the problem.

You can invoke the help of close friends if the task becomes too overwhelming for you. Having assistance will also make it easier for you to get through the experience than trying to go it alone. The support of friends and family will help.

For anything involving your college campus sites, blogs, etc. be sure to report them to the appropriate department. You should be able to find this information in your student handbook, which is most likely online.

Preventing Cyber-Bullying

Nobody asks to be bullied, yet it still can occur. However there are definitely some things you can do in order to be proactive and limit the opportunity for others to bully you.

Being responsible about your online comments, posts, tweets, etc. is the first step. The written word is a very powerful thing, but it lacks the additional information contained in voice inflection and visual aids. You may post something and think it is perfectly harmless. However, depending upon how it is worded, the person it is directed toward or about may take it out of context. Once that happens, it is very difficult to take it back or try to explain that you meant something different. Just like words that are in ALL CAPS are akin to SHOUTING, the way you phrase certain things using only words can easily be misconstrued and misunderstood.

Is there a way to be 100% certain that every single thing you comment or post online will be completely understood? Of course not. You always run the risk of not being understood regardless of whether or not someone can see and hear what you say instead of just writing it.

For this reason we have seen the rise of emoji icons. They help to convey your emotions and more clearly define your meaning. This is an additional measure that helps others know what we *really* mean, and not just say. Using textual or graphical emojis can help prevent misunderstanding, so you should use them when it is appropriate. Use them when you feel it is necessary to convey the proper mood to the recipient. If you come across in a way you didn't intend, it can come back at you in the form of harassment or cyber-bullying. Also, remember that if you bully someone else, expect it to come back at you. Don't initiate anything on purpose—it might be much worse for you!

Posting personal information, especially that which is highly sensitive or private, is a recipe for disaster. Anything that could be used to embarrass or blackmail you does not have a place online or on any public sites. Don't post anything that could potentially be used against you, because it could be. This holds true for any personal information including your address, phone number, sensitive medical information, vacation or travel plans with dates, bank or other financial information, Social Security Number, Driver's License Number, passwords, etc.

Most of this should be common sense, but a startling number of people are tricked into providing personal information on websites that are not what they purport to be. Most legitimate companies will not ask you to provide highly sensitive information; any that do should raise your suspicion. The chapter on Cyber-Security and Online Safety covers this in greater detail.

On occasion, perform online searches for yourself—you might be surprised at what you find! Hopefully there won't be anything damaging, personal or derogatory that shows up in the search results. However, it is prudent to periodically check and make sure that nothing is posted online without your knowledge. With so many people online with access to a plethora of information, it is easier than you might imagine to find and distribute information about another person. If you do find something, perform the above described methods to mitigate the problem as necessary. Remember that employers often search online to find out information about potential new hires! Be proactive!

Since *Facebook* is the largest online social media site with over 1.7 billion active monthly users (as of 2nd Qtr 2016), it is prudent that we explore some of the specific ways that you can protect yourself when using it.

First, it is imperative that you set all the Privacy settings appropriately inside of your Profile. Don't let everyone see your activity, contact information, photos, timeline, etc. Only share this with actual friends and family members. You don't want random people who may be trolling for information reaching out to you—potentially for nefarious reasons. If you receive friend requests from people you don't know or don't want to be friends with, block them.

Next, don't post anything mean about anyone. Also try to refrain from using text or images that could be misconstrued as something other than what you mean to say. Extensive use of punctuation use as "LOL!!!!" is a lot different than "lol" in the online realm. Similar uses of phrases using excessive punctuation are also not a good idea. Posting "Why did you say that?" is a lot different than "Why did you say that?!?!?" The use of capitals has already been mentioned—it is akin to SHOUTING so use sparingly, if at all. Any sort of obvious threats or bad language should be avoided at all costs. Remember, your future employer might end up reading what you post some day! If you wouldn't want them to read it, you probably shouldn't post it.

If you are bullied, harassed or receive threatening messages or posts, your first course of action is to ask the person to stop. If they do, great. If not, you will have to decide how to proceed depending upon who they are. If it is an acquaintance and you can block them, never to hear from them again, then do that. However, it will be different if it is someone that you see off-line such as a co-worker that you interact with on a professional level. Remind them they should be professional and that you do not want anything they are writing to show up on your timeline. Tell them that it is unacceptable because it could damage your professional reputation. If they don't stop, see the section above on how to proceed.

As a young adult, the things you do and say at this point in your life may sometimes be done in haste. You need to consider any potential future consequences. Ask for help from your parents or teachers if any sort of cyber-bullying is happening to you. There are things that can be done; you don't have to try and solve this problem on your own.

As mentioned before, resist the urge to retaliate . . . it may make an already bad situation worse. You will want to—badly! Don't stoop to their level and get into a back-and-forth bashing with them. It will only make you look worse, and again, remember that everything you post will remain online forever! Simply ignoring the bully is typically the best course of action.

When they realize they can't get a rise out of you, they will most likely move on to someone else.

Reporting the person to *Facebook* is always an option. *Facebook* has resources in place to combat this type of behavior. Provide them the details, they will investigate, and remove any offending posts once they determine that they should be removed. It is in *Facebook's* best interest to have a safe and fun online environment, and they take any sort of cyber-bullying and online abuse seriously. Parents can report on behalf of their children as well (http://www.facebook.com/help/?safety=parents).

In addition, you can report abuse by following this link (https://www.facebook.com/help/1417189725200547).

Reporting the person to your school's public safety or student affairs office is also a viable option if the offending behavior is being perpetrated by another student. Guidance counselors and other counselors are there to help you, so take advantage of any resources at your disposal.

The school will have polices and a student handbook. This a resource that can be referenced to determine how to handle various types of incidents. If the school is unable or unwilling to help, there is always local law enforcement. File a police report so there is a written record. Any threat involving physical violence or illegal distribution of pictures and videos, especially those that involve nudity, needs to be reported to the police immediately. Your personal safety is your number one priority, and you must take it seriously.

As a last resort with regard to eliminating cyber-bullying, you have the option of closing any affected social media or messaging accounts. Yes, it may be an inconvenience, but in the absence of other alternatives, you may have no other choice. If you're not online, you can't be cyber-bullied and you can always decide to open up a new account later once the problem has been handled.

Unfortunately the threat of bullying will always exist—both in the physical world and the online world. Taking precautions with privacy, being careful with who you interact with and what you say can go a long way toward keeping yourself safe in a digital age where information can travel just as quickly as misinformation.

Chapter 4 Checklist: Cyber-Bullying

✓ Cyber-bullying occurs when electronic devices such as cellular phones, computers & tablets are used to send text, images, or video that are intended to harass or harm someone.

✓ Cyber-bullying is typically perpetuated by online friends, classmates, ex-boyfriends or ex-girlfriends, and even by anonymous users.

✓ Any sort of messaging system can be utilized to cyberbully another person. This includes anything that is sent or posted such as information about a person's sexual orientation, ethnicity, race, weight, looks, religion or basically anything that causes someone to feel like an outcast.

✓ Using any sort of technology to record another person without their permission is another form of cyber-bullying. This includes the use of both audio and video recording devices such as cell phones and web cams.

✓ Logging in or breaking into another person's account for the purpose of sending messages or making posts while posing as that person is another illegal form of cyber-bullying.

✓ Remember: Cyber-bullying is a prosecutable crime and sometimes even just the threat of legal action can make someone stop.

✓ Any hate-related communication sent to any of your online accounts should be saved and reported to the authorities. It is no joke and constitutes a direct threat to your safety.

✓ To protect yourself, be very careful about what you say and do in the "privacy" of your home, dorm room, classroom or place of employment. There are so many video cameras out in the world today that the concept of "privacy" really no longer exists.

✓ Prevent cyber-bullying by being responsible about what you post online.

✓ Posting personal information, especially that which is highly sensitive or private is a recipe for disaster. Anything that could be used to embarrass or blackmail you, etc. does not have a place online or on any public sites.

✓ Configure privacy settings on all your online accounts to limit problems.

Cyber-Security and Online Safety

Part 1: Hackers, Phishing Scams & Identity Theft

An interconnected world opens up an entire new breed of threats to your online security. Simply having a connection to the Internet means that your computer, tablet, laptop or phone is exposed and connected to email, websites and applications—both good and bad.

Email threats exist from phishing scams and hacked, bogus email messages from people we know. They can cause us to be tricked into clicking on links where the sole purpose is to solicit your personal, financial or account information for their illegitimate gains.

The biggest threat to your online safety and security is not the innumerable hackers, countless viruses and malicious malware that exists today and will only increase in number tomorrow. <u>The biggest threat is your own complacency.</u> *Doing nothing is inviting disaster.* Thinking it is someone else's problem is a huge mistake. Systems are compromised every single day—from the largest corporate network to individual PCs. It is your responsibility, and that of your employer to block as many threats as possible. This is only done through due diligence, maintaining good habits and using common sense.

Hackers target everyone, so don't think that just because you aren't a *Fortune 500* company or a bank that hackers won't target you—they will. It is much easier for a hacker to compromise an individual user's PC or small company network. These systems typically do not have the latest security software or all the available tools that a larger corporation does. In fact, according to a 2014 report (http://www.symantec.com/security _response/publications/threatreport.jsp) by Symantec, 60% of cyber-attacks targeted small to medium size businesses.

Again, it goes back to being diligent about keeping your software up-to-date. You also must properly configure your router's firewall. If you don't know the first thing about configuring a firewall, then hire an expert who does. The small price to pay someone is trivial compared to the damage that can be done. It will be much less than the costs involved if your system is compromised by ransomware that encrypts all your files. Losing personal or company records without a current backup could be catastrophic and put a company out of business. Use a reliable backup service to keep your data safe. There are many online backup services now available—the author recommends Backup Addict (https://www.backupaddict .com/partner/idevaffiliate.php?id=103). For a flat monthly fee starting at just $14.95/month, they will remotely set it up, back up your data, provide monitoring, and help you restore it if you have a problem. Talk about peace of mind! Following this link will get you a discount that has been negotiated with them by me. Get it today and sleep better at night knowing that your valuable documents, pictures, accounting, spreadsheets, databases, presentations and more are all being backed up for you. They are also *HIPPA*-compliant, so they are a viable solution for health care companies as well.

Phishing scams have become highly sophisticated and very profitable for those perpetrating the scams. They use bulk email technology to create emails that are official looking and send them out to thousands of people. They hope that people will be fooled into acting on the emails that they receive. This is a <u>social engineering attack</u> that gets people to do something they should not. Here are some examples of these emails:

> *"It has been detected that your collegename.edu email account*
> *has been infected with a virus. Your email account is a threat to*
> *our database. You will need to update the settings on your*
> *collegename.edu email account by clicking on this link:*
> <http://forms.bogusdomain.com/form/acct_update/1234>"

"We suspect an unauthorized transaction on your bank account. To ensure that your bank account has not been compromised, please click <this link> to confirm your identity and reset your password."

"Hello, Your Amazon Prime Points are expiring—click <here> to view points.

Click <here> to hear about new Amazon products just released at unbelievable PRICES!"

These messages may sound ominous and tell you that you must act right away. If you even have the slightest doubt about the legitimacy of any messages that you receive, do NOT click the link in the message. Do not call the number in it. Instead, log into your account as you normally would and as a precaution, you should change the password.

Make sure your anti-virus software works hand-in-hand with your email program. Various programs such as *Avast, AVG, ESET, Kaspersky, McAfee, Norton* and others work to identify any malicious code trying to get into your system from emails.

The biggest threat that comes from email messages is probably ransomware at this point in time. Messages containing attachments that are zip files or executable programs wait for you to open them. Once you do, it encrypts ALL of your data files and holds them for ransom. After it runs, a message will appear on your screen telling you that all of your files have been encrypted with very strong encryption. The only way to get them back is by paying a ransom, usually in the form of untraceable *Bitcoins. (Bitcoins are a new digital currency that cannot be tracked.)*

The encryption technology used is very strong and cannot be broken. This is the fate that befell a hospital in Los Angeles, California in February 2016. All their patient records were encrypted. In the interest of getting their data back as quickly as possible, they elected to pay the ransom which they negotiated down to 40 *Bitcoins*, or around $17,000.

Experts typically recommend against paying the ransom because it empowers the criminals, provides them with funds to keep going, and validates their efforts. However, in the event that a company does not have a good, current backup, the fastest way to get back in business is to pay the ransom. *This is yet another strong argument for having a robust and working backup solution.*

Another major problem exists in a new threat, *malvertising.* Essentially, well known and trustworthy websites serve up ads that have been placed by cyber-criminals. Since the ads appear on well-known sites, they appear legitimate. However, these ads send unsuspecting visitors to websites that are designed to do a variety of things. They may sell you something you never receive or dupe you into providing certain information. They may even masquerade as another site to get your information in order to conduct identity theft.

Falling victim to identity theft can have long-term ramifications that will stay with you for a very long time and be next to impossible to rectify. Your credit will be shot as will your ability to potentially buy a house, car, get a credit card, or anything else requiring good credit.

In order to preserve your identity, one of the easiest and important things you should do is keep an eye on your credit reports. Once a year you can get a free copy from the three main credit reporting agencies (*Experian, TransUnion* and *Equifax*). You must be vigilant in ensuring that nothing shows up that you do not recognize. If you do see an inquiry or an account that you did not open, immediately contact the business or entity that is listed and find out what is going on. Any accounts that are fraudulent must be closed immediately and any entries on your credit reports challenged. You can notify the various reporting agencies and add entries to your credit report to include clarifications. Anything that has been put on as a result of identity theft should be disputed.

Also keep a close eye on your banking account statements for any strange charges or transactions that you do not recognize. They may be so small that you don't notice them such as $1.00 but course, they could be much larger. Typically a successful small charge will be followed up by subsequently larger ones as money is siphoned out of your account.

It is imperative that you keep copies of all your accounts. This includes checking, savings, credit cards, investment accounts, loans, medical records and others. This information should be kept in a secure location, preferably in a locked, fireproof safe. It should be able to be accessed immediately and your plan put into action. Plans for keeping your identity safe and for what to do in order to recover your identity are available online and easy to follow. It may not be easy to fix, however!

When paying for goods and services, keep an eye on your credit card at all times if possible. This way you are able to witness if someone tries to make a copy of your card's information. This won't always be possible, but do your best to watch your card and see where it goes. Never leave it out on your table at a restaurant or on the bar when you're running a tab.

A mistake that some people are guilty of is carrying around original copies of important documents with them such as their social security card or birth certificate. Someone with access to these original documents can essentially "become" you and open up accounts in your name. Once they do, major damage to your credit can and will occur.

One of the best websites available to help you report and recover from identity theft is https://www.identitytheft.gov/. You can also download a 68 page paper from https://www.consumer.ftc.gov/articles/pdf-0009-taking-charge.pdf that gives you specific steps on what to do if your identity is stolen.

Even well known websites can be hacked, and malicious code uploaded to them. Without the user ever knowing it, just by visiting a compromised web site and loading the page will download rogue software onto the visitor's computer. It will then carry out its task. This type of threat is very difficult to thwart, but again, anti-virus and anti-malware software that integrates with the web browser may detect it and stop the threat.

Part 2: Creating Secure Passwords

Not using secure passwords is a problem that can be fixed quickly. Unfortunately, many people choose to create passwords that are not very secure and easy to remember. These can be easily hacked using what are called *brute force attacks* with password cracking programs in a very short period of time. The challenge for people is remembering many different passwords, and so most people choose something easy to remember and use it on all their accounts. This is a major mistake. The recent news about a half a billion email accounts that were hacked at Yahoo in mid-2016 illustrates just how vulnerable these accounts are.

The strongest passwords incorporate every sort of character on the keyboard, and the longer, the better. Use a mix of capital and lower case letters, numbers, and special characters if you are able. Some systems only allow the use of letters and numbers. *In all cases, make your passwords as long as possible so they are harder to crack.* A password that is 15 characters long is much more difficult to crack than one that is only 8, usually the minimum length. Password length is more important for security than complexity, so make your passwords as long as possible.

Security experts recommend using passwords that are a minimum of 12 characters long. Basically any password that is 15 characters long or more is pretty much uncrackable. Passwords that are only 6–9 characters long are much easier to crack regardless of complexity. That is because of the time needed for a computer program to crack it. The longer the password, the more time it takes to crack. Don't put numbers at the beginning or end of your passwords as this is a very common place that most users put numbers. It is easier to remember, but also easier to hack. Keep in mind that the most common number used in passwords is not surprisingly, the number "1". The most commonly used letters are "a", "e", "o" and "r". (https://en.wikipedia.org/wiki/Password_strength #cite_note-perfect-9)

Think about this. There are commercial products that can be loaded on a standard PC, and using the higher end processor on the computer's graphics card, can test around 112,000 passwords per second!(https://en.wikipedia.org/wiki/Password _strength#cite_note-elcomsoft-5)

Another big mistake that users make is having a dictionary word in their password in one form or another. This is also not as secure as you would think since most password cracking programs take those characters into consideration when running. For example, take the word "password." Many people create variations of the word such as "pa55W0rd123" for example, and think this is secure. *Wrong!* It is almost as easy to crack as the root word (password) that was used to create it. Your best bet would be to swap out or rearrange characters and make it longer. This way, you can still pick a word to base your password on, but deviate from the word in such a way so that it is not possible to easily hack it.

For example, you could create the password "5%w0dP8r 4&9#Wr7". This is *infinitely* stronger, and makes it *many* times more difficult to crack. It uses no dictionary words of any combination and it is 15 characters long. I used the root word as a starting point, but as you can see, the end result looks nothing like the root word, "password". Of course, the problem with creating such complex passwords becomes *remembering* the passwords we create! This is why there is such a problem with people's accounts being compromised . . . they do not do this because it is too much of a hassle, too difficult to remember, or both.

Another no-no when it comes to password creation is repeating the same character in the password, either back-to-back or even at all. Studies have shown that the majority of people's passwords use only 32 different characters and certain characters are used almost all the time.

Also, do not repeat sequences of characters on the keyboard, such as "5678" or "asdf" since password cracking programs try those combinations during hacking attempts.

Other pieces of information that are readily available about you should also not be used. This includes your birthday, your anniversary, your kids' names, your pet's name, your street or house number, zodiac sign, etc. These are all things that can easily be found out about you on social media or directory sites. If the information is out there, and you use it, it can and will be used against you. Don't use any of it!

Something that almost everyone is guilty of is using the same password more than once. Many users pick a password (usually one that is easy to remember and thus, not secure) and use it across *all* of their accounts, programs, websites, etc. Think about how easy it would be for a hacker to infiltrate *all* of your accounts and gain access to everything if they hack your password! When they try it on your other accounts, they discover (to their joy) that it is the same everywhere! If you have multiple online banking and investing accounts, the hacker just gained access to all your money! Imagine the sinking feeling in the pit of your stomach if you were to wake up one day and discover that all your money in all of your accounts is gone. It is enough to make people consider desperate and disturbing things . . . so don't let it happen to you!

So how are you supposed to remember all of these super complex and nearly impossible to hack account passwords? Some experts recommend not writing them down, while others say it's OK if you keep them secure. The author (who is also an IT consultant) has three recommendations.

First, everyone carries a cell phone and they can be locked. If you store your passwords in your phone, and the phone is locked with a PIN, swipe pattern or fingerprint, then technically you can keep them secure. You usually have your phone with you all the time. However, the problem with this is what happens if your phone is stolen? What happens if your phone breaks and you can no longer access it? What about if you forget your cell phone password? Just be sure backup your phone regularly!

A second option is to enter them into a spreadsheet or database on your computer and password protect or encrypt the file. Keep several backup copies of the file so that if something happens to your computer, you still have a copy of this critical file. You can use an online storage service like *Dropbox* or *iCloud* to backup your files automatically in real-time which can be a lifesaver. Other options like the Backup Addict (https://www.backupaddict.com/partner/idevaffiliate.php?id= 103), *Carbonite*, *SpiderOak*, *Acronis* and others can also be utilized for your peace of mind. They are not just for keeping your password file safe and secure, but all of your data files. *Here is my personal recommendation.* Keep all your account information in a password protected database. Then, back it up daily using an on-line backup service. In addition, back it up to an *off-line* hard drive weekly. That way, there is no way you will ever lose it!

The third option is to remove the digital complications completely from the mix. This means physically writing down all your account information including user names and passwords. Keep them in a secure location such as a locked desk drawer or safe. There is no file to get corrupted, phone to be stolen or computer to crash, but there is no such thing as 100% secure. If you keep a paper record in a wooden desk drawer and a fire burns your office down, obviously you have just lost those passwords—along with a lot of other things!

The best thing is to be vigilant, careful and if at all possible, keep your sensitive account information secure in *whatever way works best for you*. There is no right or wrong answer, but find the method you are most comfortable with and use it. *The best backup is the one that you have.*

Part 3: Software Upgrades and Patches

Ignoring software patch and update notifications from various software manufacturers on your computer is another potential problem. People feel that they can't be bothered or are too busy to install updates when they become available. This is a huge mistake that can lead to having a system or phone with major security flaws. They can and will be exploited by hackers. It is imperative to install updates to your programs, applications and operating system as soon as you are able to. Keep your devices up-to-date with the latest and most secure and patched versions of their software.

The reason that manufacturers release updates is to improve the functionality or the security of their programs. They don't release updates without good reason, and so you should not ignore them. Even if a release simply adds functionality and does nothing for security, you may benefit from the enhancement. Security updates and software patches are essential because if programs and systems are left vulnerable, the data on that system becomes vulnerable and that presents a risk to your personal safety and security. *Install updates as soon as possible.*

As mentioned before, information that is released without your knowledge can cause damage to you in many ways. Relationships can be put as risk, your finances can be compromised, or your employment could be jeopardized. These are just a few of the reasons why you simply must act on alerts from various vendors about the availability of updates. Some are extremely important such as those involving online programs including your anti-virus program, email software and browser. These are the programs on the "front lines" that you use to interact with the Internet on a daily basis. *Ignoring essential updates could be a huge mistake if the update contains fixes for security vulnerabilities.*

Keep in mind that hackers often don't even know about a vulnerability until an update is released by the company. They review the update log to see what the update "fixed." Then, using that information they can attempt to hack into or exploit systems that have not installed the update yet! This is a way of "reverse hacking" that is used to quickly find machines that have not yet applied the fix. When they do, they can now do their dirty deeds and use the machine as they wish. They may hack into it and obtain user data, use it as a server to send out spam or copies of itself, or even to distribute pornography or viruses.

There are many measures that you can take to make your online experience safer. Using pop-up ad blockers and anti-malware software can go a long way toward securing your computer. Be sure to look at and configure your browser's cookie settings, history and privacy settings. Everything that you can do that increases your privacy and security will make your personal information safer.

The bottom line: Keep your technology updated and apply all fixes immediately to keep you as safe and secure as possible!

Part 4: Cyber-Crime

Another piece of the cyber-security puzzle involves cyber-crime. Cyber-crime encompasses a variety of online crimes. This includes the theft of information, music, movies, and money. Everyone from individual hackers to foreign governments are guilty of various forms of cyber-crime. Spying on other countries by hacking their accounts is nothing new. The sheer volume and proliferation of information makes it simple to share data at lightening speed—legally or not. This presents a huge problem for the music and movie industries which have seen major losses due to illegal distribution of songs and movies.

If you illegally download movies, songs, videos, television shows or other commercial content from various "torrent" sites, you are breaking the law. In addition, many of these sites also install malware, key loggers, Trojan horses and spyware on your computer when you download these hacked media files. Pirated software presents a security risk to not only your computer but also your personal information.

The number of cyber-crimes has exploded in recent years as the technology necessary to hack systems has evolved. A recent survey by the National Small Business Association (http://www.nbsa.biz/) found that 1 out of 2 businesses surveyed had reported being victims of cyber-attacks. During one month in 2015, 3 out of 4 phishing attacks targeted small businesses with 250 employees or less. The average cost of a cyber-attack is around $21,000. Even more disturbing is that within 6 months of a cyber-attack, 60% of those attacked go out of business. These are startling statistics that illustrate just how severe the problem is.

With regard to individual systems, they are still part of a larger network. When you are on your college wifi, you are connected to their network, which is in turn connected to the Internet. You are just as vulnerable to a cyber-attack as any other machine on their network. You may not think of the college as a business, but it most certainly is. It contains lots of sensitive information that a hacker would love to get their hands on such as names, addresses, social security numbers, and financial aid documents. Other data may disclose incomes and investments, employee salary information, donor and alumni information and much more.

The threat cannot be overstated, and it is up to you as an individual to ensure that your system is as up-to-date as possible as discussed in the section above. Having secure passwords and keeping your anti-virus software and anti-malware program running and up-to-date can go a long way toward securing your data. If you are unsure how to proceed or need help, don't be afraid to contact your college's desktop support department. Ask them to help you make sure that your computer is as secure as possible. You can even ask what measures are being taken to secure their network from hackers and threats.

It is important that you feel comfortable with what you do when you are online on any network. This includes at home, school, work, the airport, the local coffee shop or public wifi hotspot. The more networks you connect to, the more vulnerable you become simply because you are exposing your data to more systems. If any of those are not secured well or have a compromised machine on them, you risk a potential problem. Do you really think that every college student's computer, phone, and tablet is secure? It is because of this that you must do everything possible to ensure that your individual computer is as secure as it can be. Hire a professional if necessary! The cost to secure your computer pales in comparison to the costs if your personal data is compromised—either from the standpoint of identity theft or from a financial standpoint.

With the rise of credit and debit cards containing "chips" (Radio Frequency Identifiers or RFIDs) there is another digital threat to your personal safety and security. *Electronic* or *digital pickpocketing* is the digital form of traditional pickpocketing, except the criminal never has to touch you. Other types of cards such as ID cards with RFIDs can also be read and compromised, and this data can then be used to create bogus cards that can be used to access secure areas such as banks, pharmacies, and businesses that utilize RFID technology on their ID badges.

You may not have heard about this new threat, but with all the hype about how these new chipped credit cards are supposed to keep our data safer, *they actually can be compromised more easily.* All these criminals need to do is position themselves and their scanning equipment (which can simply be an app on a smartphone or tablet) near you and your wallet with these new chip cards in it. They may simply bump up against you on the subway, in an elevator, or behind you while you're in line at the store. The app on their tablet or smartphone can read the RFID being emitted from your new "secure" credit card contained in this new chip.

The app reads the card number, expiration date and personal information right off the card. Now all the thief needs to do is use it to make purchases online and ship the products to their address, which is typically a box location such as a PO Box, *UPS Store* or *FedEx Store*.

This is a scary proposition, since the guise being put forth is that these cards contain chips in order to make us safer and keep our identity more secure. *Unfortunately, this isn't the case.*

So how do you secure these new "chipped" credit and debit cards that now number more than ten million? There are ways to prevent them from being read. The cheap, low-tech version is to simply wrap the cards in tinfoil. This prevents the chip from being read by one of this scanning apps. Another method is to insert the chip cards into a card sleeve that has a metal case around it to prevent the card inside from being scanned. This is a good solution if you only have one or two cards with these RFID chips. Sleeves are also available for ID badges and passports, since new passports now contain RFID chips in them.

If you have a lot of cards with RFID chips, there are shielded clutches and wallets that will protect all the RFID cards inside. Other types of shielded sleeves and holders are available to protect you and keep your data secure.

Part 5: Cyber-Terrorism

Cyber-terrorism can be defined across a wide spectrum of activities. It typically is explained as the use of the Internet to conduct terrorist acts. Terrorism by definition is conducted to create terror in the intended victims. Therefore, by extrapolation, cyber-terrorism is the use of the Internet to facilitate the striking of terror in the victim. This fact is what separates cyber-terrorism from cyber-war or cyber-crime.

Sending malware and viruses across the Internet with the purpose of disrupting computers and networks is one way that terrorist organizations conduct cyber-terror attacks. These disruptions can include relatively benign "distributed denial of service" attack (DDoS). These cause little more than a temporary inconvenience for the target by disrupting their website, email and Internet connection. Much more damaging attacks have a defined purpose like shutting down critical infrastructure such as electricity distribution centers. They could also cause other systems to malfunction and perhaps overheat or explode. If people are injured or killed as a result of cyber-terrorism, that would complete the objective of striking terror in the hearts of the intended victims, their families, co-workers, etc.

Cyber-terrorism can also involve politically or economically motivated hacking by individuals or groups. Their purpose is causing economic or physical damage including injury or death to others. This can include the sending out of electronic communications which contain damaging or misleading information. It can also include creating websites for the purposes of spreading ideologies or propaganda. Hacked websites that redirect to alternate pages displaying messages are another form of cyber-terrorism that occurs fairly regularly. From business to government sites, hacker groups often use this tactic as a way to bring attention to movements or bad business practices. While it does not necessarily cause terror, it no doubt has an impact on those it affects.

One extreme example of cyber-terrorism would be to hack into a nuclear power plant's computer control system. The hacker could modify cooling settings which could lead to a catastrophic meltdown of the core. Not only would this cause terror, but there would be potential injuries and deaths as a result.

Chapter 5 Checklist:
Cyber-Security and Online Safety

✓ Simply having a connection to the Internet means that your computer, tablet, laptop or phone is exposed. You are connected to email, websites and applications—both good and bad.

✓ Email threats in the form of phishing scams and hacked, bogus email messages from people we know can cause us to be lured into visiting websites. Clicking on hyperlinks takes you to a site designed to solicit your personal, financial or account information for their illegitimate gains.

✓ *The biggest threat to your online safety and security is your own complacency. This is only corrected through due diligence, maintaining good online habits and using common sense.*

✓ Use a reliable backup service to keep your data safe. Be sure that your anti-virus software works hand-in-hand with your email. The biggest threat that comes in from email messages is ransomware at this point. These programs use encryption technology that is very strong and cannot be broken. Do not click on any email attachment and make sure your anti-virus software is up-to-date and scans everything.

✓ Falling victim to identity theft can have long-term ramifications that will stay with you for a very long time and be next to impossible to rectify. Your credit will be shot as will your ability to potentially buy a house, car, get a credit card, or anything else requiring good credit. Be sure to shred all paper records with your name, account numbers, bills, insurance policies, medical records and anything else that can identify you.

✓ The strongest passwords incorporate every sort of character on the keyboard, and the longer, the better. Basically any password that is 15 characters long or more is pretty much uncrackable. Passwords that are only 6–9 characters long are much easier to crack regardless of complexity.

✓ It is imperative to install updates to your programs, applications and operating system as soon as you are able in order to keep your devices up-to-date with the latest and most secure and patched versions. You must do everything possible to ensure that your individual computer is as secure as it can be, especially if you connect to many different networks.

✓ Protect your credit cards, IDs and anything that contain RFIDs.

CHAPTER 6

Social Media and Cell
Phone Do's & Don'ts

Part 1: Social Media Behavior

Social media is a powerful tool that can have both positive and negative effects on our lives. The variety of sites is staggering with sites like *Facebook, Twitter, YouTube, Instagram, Snap-Chat* and others that boast millions and millions of worldwide users.

On the positive side, social media keeps us connected with friends and family. We can stay in touch, look at pictures and watch videos of our friends on vacation or of their children growing up. When others are far away, the Internet and social media can make them seem closer to us and the distances melt away.

On the negative side, it can be used against you in a variety of ways. You must be extremely careful when posting any information about you, your family, your friends or your school. Anything you post exists online forever. Just because you delete a post doesn't mean it is really gone; it exists on backups. If you post something negative about a friend, you can be sure that it will make its way back to them in short order. When they confront you about it, either online or offline, it will be extremely awkward to say the least. Many a friendship has been ruined by social media; don't ruin any of your friendships by posting things that you will regret in the future.

It is also imperative that you search for yourself occasionally in order to keep tabs on what others may be posting about you.

You might be surprised at what you find! It is important to find any negative posts about you and deal with them swiftly. Social media sites have departments that deal with abuse and negative posts. Report any derogatory or malicious content as soon as you discover it so you limit the damage to your reputation and possible future implications.

Specifically with regard to employment, many employers look up employees online to see what they can learn from their online presence. Are they posting and promoting politically charged topics? Are they bashing their boss or their company? How about their comments in general? Are they positive people or complainers? Your conduct on social media tells people a lot about you. Make sure you are portraying yourself online in the way that you want others to see you.

Part 2: Cell Phone Safety Tips

Cellular phones have become so much more than simple phones—they have morphed into *smartphones*. These mini touch-screen computers do much more than simply make phone calls. They send texts, images, and videos to other phones and enable us to video conference. We can search the Internet and check email. The pictures they take rival high-end cameras. We can conduct stock trades and monitor our investments in real time. They enable us to monitor our health as well as the weather. Our phones store our contacts, track our schedules, and take dictation for us. We can use them as media devices to read books, play games, watch movies, and listen to music. They function as GPS systems and guide us to our destinations. They can act as a flashlight, function as a personal safety device and do so much more. The amount of things they can do is staggering and it is constantly increasing. *They have become useful devices that we simply cannot live without.*

It is because of all of these things that makes them our Achilles Heel in many ways. Take the smart phone off of a teenager or young adult and they are unable to function! The concept of *(gasp!)* spending even just a few hours without it can be sheer torture! *What makes these devices dangerous is that they have desensitized us to the world around us in a bad way.* They take so much of our attention that they distract us from things around us that may be important to notice but we don't. Our senses can be affected negatively in such as way that our safety may be compromised. <u>This is unacceptable and you need to understand this.</u>

Your **hearing** can be compromised if your earbuds are in and the music is playing too loud. You may not hear the commotion around the next corner, someone screaming or police sirens nearby. You may find yourself walking toward something or someone when you should be running away! If you can't hear it, you can't react and by the time you notice, it may be too late to do anything. *Don't become a victim or jeopardize your personal safety from something as easy to correct as not playing your music so loudly that you drown out all outside noises.*

Your **vision** can be compromised by looking at your bright screen in the dark where it destroys your night vision. Turn the brightness on your smartphone down as low as you can stand it so that it has the least effect on your night vision. The newest smartphones have a "blue light" filter that helps you see better at night. If you have trouble seeing, you may not notice the person or persons who are approaching you until it is too late! Not being able to see is obviously something that puts you at a major disadvantage. Train yourself to look up frequently whenever you find yourself staring at the phone's screen for more than few minutes. It only takes seconds to look up and survey your surroundings. However, it also only takes seconds for someone to sneak up on you. Be aware of the time you spend before looking up from your screen—it just may save your life.

You are probably guilty of one or both of these behaviors that can be attributed to frequent smartphone use. There is no reason why you have to be looking down at your phone constantly when walking down the road, crossing streets, or going in-between classes on campus. You could walk into another person, an object such as a tree or lamp post, trip on an uneven sidewalk or fail to step up or down a curb. All these present threats to your personal safety, but they are not the most dangerous problems that can arise.

The most dangerous problems are those of a direct physical threat to your personal safety from someone bent on doing you harm. It could be one or more individuals looking to rob you of your wallet, phone and jewelry or it could be worse. There could be a group interested in sexually assaulting you and perhaps killing you after they are done. *This is an extreme example, but one that needs to be mentioned since everyone is not your friend.* Keep in mind that serial murderers are often well-dressed, groomed and polite individuals when you first meet them so that they gain your trust. Then, they become the face of true evil and will stop at nothing to achieve their goals—no matter how terrible they may be. **Chapter 13** provides real-world solutions for physical threats to your personal safety.

Chapter 6 Checklist: Social Media & Cell Phone Do's & Don'ts

✓ You must be extremely careful when posting any information about you, your family, your friends or your school. Anything you post exists online forever. Many a friendship has been ruined by social media; don't ruin any of your friendships by posting things that you will regret in the future.

✓ Search for yourself occasionally in order to keep tabs on what others may be posting about you . . . you might be surprised at what you find! It is important to find any negative posts about you and deal with them swiftly.

✓ What makes cell phones dangerous is that they have desensitized us from the world around us in a bad way. They take so much of our attention that they distract us from things around us that may be important to notice but don't. Your senses can be affected negatively in such as way that your safety may be compromised.

✓ Your **hearing** can be compromised if your earbuds are in and the music is loudly playing.

✓ Your **vision** can be compromised by looking at your bright screen in the dark where it destroys your night vision.

✓ Train yourself to look up frequently whenever you find yourself staring at the phone's screen for more than a few minutes. It only takes seconds to look up and survey your surroundings.

CHAPTER 7

Alcohol Responsibility / Party Drugs / Prescription Medication Abuse

College is a time for growing up and experiencing new things. One of the areas that most college students experiment with is alcohol. At some point in your college career, and most likely throughout your college career, you will attend parties where alcohol is served. There may also be other things at these parties including illegal drugs and so-called "party drugs." All of these will impair your judgment and ability to make proper decisions. It is one thing to drink legal alcohol, whether or not you are of legal age. It is an entirely different situation when you use illegal drugs, and even worse if you are given illegal drugs or medication without your knowledge.

Part 1: Alcohol Responsibility

In many ways, college and drinking are linked because of fraternity and sorority parties, toga parties, costume parties and parties just to party! The association has been drilled home by movies as well, which always seem to depict college students as heavy drinkers. It is true that many college students will drink and get drunk for the first time in their lives at college, and it is considered by some to be a rite of passage. According to a *2013 National Survey on Drug Use and Health*, almost 60% of college students between 18–22 drank alcohol in the last month, and almost 40% had been "binge" drinking in that same time period. Binge drinking as defined in the survey was 4–5 drinks in 2 hours whereby the blood alcohol content (BAC) reached or exceeded 0.08 g/dL. *Drinking to excess is where problems begin to occur, and continues to be a significant problem on campuses.*

So exactly what constitutes a "drink?" According to the Centers for Disease Control and Prevention (CDC; http://www.cdc .gov/alcohol/fact-sheets/alcohol-use.htm), in the United States, an alcoholic drink contains 0.6 oz of pure alcohol. This is the amount contained in:

- 12oz beer with 5% alcohol content
- 8oz malt liquor with 8% alcohol content
- 5oz wine with 12% alcohol content
- 1.5oz 80-proof liquor with 40% alcohol content

Excessive drinking is defined as four drinks at a time for women or five drinks at a time for men. Heavy drinking is defined at eight or more drinks per week for women, or 15 or more drinks per week for men. Moderate drinking is one drink per day for women or two drinks per day for men. For a comprehensive listing, visit www.alcoholcontents.com.

Drinking large amounts of alcohol in a short period of time such as when you are playing drinking games, doing "keg stands" or shotgunning beers, is not only going to get you drunk. It is going to impair your ability to think clearly and you will make poor decisions. You will forget things, become careless and lose inhibitions. Some of these may not be so bad, but others can be devastating. Imagine these scenarios:

1. You decide to "catch a buzz" before going out to a party. As a result, you forget to lock the door to your dorm room when you leave. When you return hours later, you discover either that night or the next morning when you wake up that things are missing. Where is your laptop? What happened to your new shoes?
2. You and some friends decide to do some shots in the early afternoon before heading out to the school's football game. You leave your apartment but forget to blow out the candle that is burning on the coffee table. While at the game, you hear sirens and think nothing of it. Upon returning to your apartment you find that the candle you left unattended burned down and set the coffee table on fire, which in turn set the carpet on fire and

eventually the rest of your small apartment. Everything is gone.

3. It's a Wednesday night and you decide to take a break from studying for a big exam you have the next day. Your roommates convince you to go out "just for a drink or two." Well, a couple turns into a lot more, and before you realize it, you're wasted. The next thing you remember is waking up . . . after the test is over!

4. You're at a party with some of your girlfriends. Everyone is having a good time and drinking some concoction they're calling "jungle juice". As the night progresses, many of your friends get pretty drunk and start "hooking up." Before you know it, you're alone with a few guys and the next thing you know, you wake up hours later and can't remember anything. Your clothes are half off, your hair is a wreck and you have no idea where you are.

Let's take a closer look at each of these four scenarios.

1. In the first one, forgetfulness as a result of drinking caused you to not lock your door and as a result, your laptop and expensive shoes are stolen.

2. In the second, excessive alcohol consumption before going to a football game distracted you from making sure that your apartment was safe and secure. An unattended candle burned all your belongings as a result.

3. The third scenario causes a direct, negative effect on your grade since by drinking to excess, you passed out and missed a major test. Try explaining that to your professor!

4. The fourth scenario is the scariest; the victim has a drink laced with a drug known as GHB or "Easy Lay" on the streets. This date rape drug caused the victim to be raped and remember nothing.

Later in this chapter are further explanations about various date rape drugs, the forms they come in and the effects on their victims. For now, we will take a closer look at alcohol.

Simply drinking to excess without the presence of any other drug can result in risky sexual behavior. This includes doing things that a person normally would not do in a sober state. Having sex with someone you typically would not, having unprotected sex, or performing sexual acts you normally would not do. Even having sex with multiple partners are all potential behaviors that could be the result of lowered sexual inhibitions as a result of drinking.

While we're on the topic of sex, it is imperative that if you are sexually active, you protect yourself and your partner by using a barrier like a condom. College can be a time of sexual exploration and even promiscuity to a certain extent. The more partners you have, the greater your chances of catching a sexually transmitted disease (STD). In fact, according to the *American Social Health Organization*, one in four teens becomes infected with an STD each year, so you've got a pretty good chance of catching one if you're not careful!

STDs range from herpes and genital warts (human papilloma virus or HPV) to more serious diseases such as Hepatitis, Chlamydia, Syphilis, Gonorrhea (the "Clap") and the most deadly of them all, AIDS. Symptoms can include a rash, sores, bumps, severe itching, discharge, painful urination, and flu-like symptoms (fever, chills, aches). If you suspect that you may have an STD, see your doctor immediately!

For more in-depth information regarding STDs, WebMD (http://www.webmd.com/) is a good place to start http://www.webmd.com/sexual-conditions/guide/sexual-health-stds#1. Another excellent resource is https://www.womenshealth.gov/.

A startling fact uncovered by Colombia University's National Center on Addiction and Substance Abuse (http://www.centeronaddiction.org/) found that 90% of rapes on college campuses involve alcohol. A study on campus rape that was published in the Journal of American College Health (http://www.acha.org/ACHA/Resources/Topics/Violence.aspx?WebsiteKey=03f1a0d5-4c58-4ff4-9b6b-764854022ac1) found that 73% of assailants and 55% of rape victims used alcohol or other drugs prior to the assault.

Alcohol in excess can have a very pronounced effect on a person's demeanor. If you have ever witnessed a violent drunk, you know exactly what this means. Alcohol affects different people in different ways. Some people get very relaxed and agreeable, but other people get unreasonable and violent. You cannot reason with an unreasonable drunk—don't waste your time and energy! Simply stay away from them.

Another huge problem with frequent alcohol consumption or excessive drinking is the effect it can have on your schoolwork. There is the potential to produce poor quality work, miss classes and fall behind. College is a huge investment in your future; you don't want to jeopardize it by making poor decisions as a result of drinking to excess on a regular basis. Being highly intoxicated also deadens your senses. This could prove to be fatal in the event of a fire or other emergency. If you sleep or are passed out through a fire alarm that ends up being an actual fire (and not just burnt popcorn) you could lose your life.

Part 2: Alcohol-Related Health Issues

On the topic of sleep, passing out is not the same as quality sleep. Drinking alcohol interferes with your body's ability to get restful sleep. The result is that you do not get proper rest. You will feel like crap, and probably begin to look like crap too! Others may notice this and wonder what is happening. This could affect your social interactions with your family, friends, girlfriend/boyfriend, teachers and classmates.

Alcohol dehydrates you, and this results in the "hangover" that you feel after a night of excessive drinking. The effects of this dehydration over the long term can affect your skin and deprive it of the hydration it needs to stay elastic and look good. No one wants premature wrinkles, so stay hydrated! The dehydrating affects of alcohol on the skin often exacerbates the affects of eczema, acne and rosacea. If you're wondering why your face is breaking out, take a look at how much you're drinking!

There is a notion that drinking helps you to relax and reduce stress. Although this may be true in some people, in others the exact opposite occurs. In these people, drinking can cause additional stress. Excessive alcohol consumption may have a very negative effect on your health. This can occur either directly or indirectly. Excessive consumption of alcohol may result in everything from missing class to alcohol poisoning or worse. It can affect your health if you injure yourself as a result of a fall or because you were unaware of a threat such as being struck by a car.

Alcohol poisoning is another result of excessive alcohol consumption. Contrary to popular belief, it does not take multiple times to get alcohol poisoning—it can occur the first time if you drink too much. Don't think you can't drink yourself to death, because it can happen. If you drink alcohol without realizing how much in a short period of time, this is a sure-fire formula for big problems. This can happen especially if you have mixed drinks where you cannot taste the alcohol. Punches and juices blended with grain alcohol can have devastating results on anyone. Since you can't taste the alcohol, you don't realize how strong it is. You drink more and more until you black out, pass out, throw up or worse. Alcohol poisoning can affect your breathing, heart rate, body temperature and gag reflex and can result in coma or death. Symptoms of alcohol poisoning include slurred speech, confusion, loss of coordination, vomiting, irregular breathing, pale or blue-tinged skin or becoming unresponsive or unconscious.

If you suspect alcohol poisoning, immediate medical attention is required. Call 911 and be prepared to give the dispatcher as many details as possible such as what the person was drinking and how much you think they had. If you do not know, tell them you are unsure. Do not leave the person unattended; if they vomit and are unconscious, they could choke on their own vomit and die. Try to keep them conscious and upright or at least laying on their side. The person may need to be given oxygen or intravenous fluids consisting of glucose and vitamins. They may possibly even need something called *hemodialysis* which involves using a machine to rapidly filter the alcohol out of the person's blood.

Long-term health risks can also arise from excessive alcohol consumption. A variety of heart-related problems such as high blood pressure, heart disease, stroke, liver disease, kidney failure and digestive issues can all occur. Various types of cancer can also develop including cancer of the throat, esophagus, mouth, liver and colon. Learning and memory issues may surface as a result which would directly affect your schoolwork.

Mental health issues including anxiety and depression can also develop as a result of excessive drinking. Problems with family and friends may begin to manifest themselves. Alcoholism could end up being the result of your drinking habits, and that is a big problem that would affect all areas of your life. *The bottom line is to keep your drinking in check!* For more information, see the World Health Organization's 2014 global status report (http://www.who.int/substance_abuse/publications/global_alcohol_report/en/) on alcohol and health.

Alcohol is a big factor in motor vehicle fatalities by college students and recent college graduates. Approximately 30% of drivers who died in 2014 between the ages of 21–24 had a blood alcohol level over the legal limit.

In fact, excessive alcohol use is responsible for approximately 88,000 deaths per year, and 1 in 10 deaths of adults between the ages of 25–64.

If you are caught driving under the influence and are under 21, you might immediately lose your license in many states for 6 months to a year. That could have a huge effect on your life. You may be unable to get to work. More importantly, it can result in injury or death for you or others.

You don't have to be in an accident to be permanently affected by an alcohol-related traffic citation. A DUI can cost you your license as well as a lot of money in court costs, fines, and increased car insurance rates. In addition, it becomes a part of your permanent record which can have devastating consequences on your future employment. Many employers look at driving records when reviewing job applications. A DUI, even if you don't need to drive for your job, could affect you being hired. Think about it. If a job is between you and another person and everything is pretty much equal with regard to education and work experience, but you have a DUI and the other applicant does not, what do you think an employer would do?

What happens if a subsequent DUI gets your license to drive suspended? How would you get to your job? If you drive for your job, you would be unable to complete the function that you were hired to perform and most likely be fired. Don't discount how serious moving violations and DUIs can be on your ability to get and keep a job both now and in the future!

The bottom line: *Don't drink and drive regardless of whether you are under or over 21 years of age.*

On the topic of legal drinking age, do not provide alcohol to minors if you are over 21. This is a serious crime that can get you in major trouble with the law. If the minor is involved in a DUI accident, the result could be a felony charge levied against the person who provided them with the alcohol. A felony conviction becomes a part of your permanent record, and again, this could affect your current or future employment.

Another serious problem that can arise out of being drunk is getting into fights. Maybe you said something you shouldn't have when you had "loose lips," or you get argumentative with the wrong person. Whatever the reason, if you are charged with assault, you may end up with a felony charge that will remain on your permanent record. *Simply having a felony, any felony, on your record could prevent you from being hired from certain jobs that require a clean record for employment.* It would be terrible for you to lose out on a great job in the future because of a stupid mistake you made in your youth.

Part 3: Bar and Club Safety

The most important rule of going out is to never go out alone. If you do, then you will be most likely drinking and driving unless you are taking public transportation or a taxi. However, it is a good rule of thumb to always have someone with you. It is also a good idea to let others know where you are going and when to expect you back. This is an additional measure of safety that could have significant importance if something does happen to you while you are out.

The next most important rule is to regulate your alcohol consumption. Know what is too much and recognize when you have had too much to drink. This simple precaution can keep you out of trouble since bad things tend to happen when people drink to excess. The more drunk you become, the easier target you are to predators and criminals. By staying in control of how much you drink, you will be less likely to deviate from your normal behavior and this will keep you safer. Know your limits and what you can safely consume.

Something else to consider is your intended destination. What is the reputation for where you want to go? Is there a history of trouble at the establishment? If so, you may want to go elsewhere. What about parking? Do you have to walk a distance between where you have to park and the club? If it is a reputable club with video surveillance, large security presence and no history òf trouble, you should feel pretty comfortable going there. If they have close-by, adequate and well-lit parking, this is important to consider as well. Use your head, and make informed decisions. If you do, this will take you a long way toward staying out of trouble. Have a main plan for getting home as well as a backup plan. Be sure that you keep enough money for a cab ride home should you need one—just in case.

Another big mistake that is made when going out is neglecting to eat a good meal. Saying you don't want to fill up before going out is nonsense! Drinking on an empty stomach is not smart—period. The alcohol you consume will go straight into your bloodstream and not be absorbed more slowly by the food in your belly. Even a quick bite before going out will help. Don't get sucked in to drinking more than you planned because someone is buying your drinks. You may be tempted to get a drink every time one is offered, but if you are at your limit or you find yourself drinking too fast or getting buzzed, slow down! It's OK to say no if a drink is offered to you. Many times, the person buying you the drink may have ulterior motives.

On the topic of ulterior motives, never under any circumstances leave your drink unattended. There may be any number of reasons why you want to or have to leave your drink. Maybe you have to run out to your car, go to the bathroom, or make a phone call outside. If you can't trust your friends to watch it for you, ask the bartender to put it behind the bar for you until you return. Leaving your drink unattended is a recipe for disaster. This is when the time is ripe for someone to slip something into it without your knowledge. At all times keep your drink in view and in front of you. It only takes a fraction of a second for someone to put something in your drink. If you think that your drink smells odd or tastes funny, discard it immediately and do not drink it! You can always get another one.

When you get a mixed drink, watch it being made by the bartender and keep your eyes on it until it gets to you. Do not accept a drink from anyone but the bartender if you can help it. Do not accept a drink from a stranger, especially one that is either in a cup or an open bottle. An unopened bottle would be the only drink that is most likely safe to drink, but in all honesty, how do you know that the screw-top bottle cap wasn't put back on after a drug was slipped into it. The answer is—you don't.

If you are a woman and going to a bar where it's "Ladies Night" and women drink for free—beware! Not only is it easy for you to drink more than you intend to, it is a place sure to be frequented by those looking for their next target or victim. Be vigilant and make smart decisions. Just because the drinks are free doesn't mean you can drink more than you should. If you do, you will be compromising your personal safety and security by becoming an easier target both for rape and robbery.

Going to a bar or club that doesn't have a lot of people can be a drag . . . but going to a bar or club that is so packed you can barely move presents a real threat to your safety. Being unable to freely move is important in the event you need to vacate the premises quickly such as in a fire. If you cannot easily move about, you are going to be at greater risk. Places that are overcrowded also tend to get people annoyed. When someone can't get to the bar or the bathroom and when alcohol and pissed off people mix, the results are usually not good. In addition, it is much easier to rob someone in a crowded area since it is much easier to do a "snatch and grab" of a purse or wallet and then disappear into the crowd. Keep your valuables close at hand. According to the *US State Department*, pick-pockets and purse snatchers are most active in very crowded places. They also advise that you keep your money or other items of value in a front pocket.

Women who are intoxicated are more likely to be assaulted or the victim of rape. If you are a woman, take this advice to heart and don't make the mistake of getting so drunk that you are unaware of your surroundings or have a "black out" episode where you don't remember events that occurred while you were drunk.

Part 4: Party Drugs, Energy Drinks and Prescription Medication Abuse

College students may try drugs for a variety of reasons. These may include stress relief, staying awake to work, study or party, and pressure from their peers. Altering your mental and physical state can be accomplished with so-called party drugs and the abuse of prescription medications. Both are illegal if not prescribed to you, and can have serious affects on your body, mind and overall health. Any sort of first-time exposure to drugs will have an unknown affect on you. Repeated exposure can result in addiction and major health problems.

Party Drugs (Date Rape Drugs)

The use of date-rape drugs cannot be underestimated. Many types exist and have different affects on the victim, so be extremely careful about keeping an eye on your drink at parties and at the bar. It only takes a split second for someone to slip a drug into a drink. The three most common date-rape or "club drugs" are Rohypnol (ruffies/rope/R-2/mind erasers), GHB—short for gamma hydroxybutyric (Easy Lay, Energy Drink, G, G-juice, liquid X) and Ketamine (Black Hole, Bump, Jet, K, Special K, Purple).

All of these drugs are powerful and fast-acting. *Mixing them with alcohol makes them even more potent.* Date rape drugs are designed to assist the perpetrator of a sexual assault by allowing them to do something the victim would not normally agree to. This includes inappropriate touching, rape, sexual intercourse, putting something including foreign objects into the vagina or anus, and attempted rape. Most of these drugs have no taste, no color, and no smell which makes them impossible to detect. They make the person weak, confused or simply pass out so that the victim is unable to refuse the advances or defend themselves. They can be used to rob a victim by having them pass out and easier to rob, but the typical use is for sexual assault on both females *and* males.

As introduced above, there are four main types of date rape drugs. The first, Rohypnol (*flunitrazepam*) is one of the most popular and two forms of it have been showing up in the United States. The next is called Klonopin (*clonazapam*). The third one that you may have heard of is Xanax (*alprazolam*). Finally, a drug that was popular in the 1990s has come back in popularity—Ecstasy (*3,4-Methylenedioxy-methamphet imine*). This party drug is very often abused by teens and young adults. It is commonly found at concerts and raves.

Rohypnol goes by a variety of names on the street including Circles, Forget Pill, Ruffies, Rope, R-2, Mind Erasers, Roofies, Roach, Lunch Money, Rib and others. It comes as a pill that dissolves in liquids, making it easy to slip into the drinks of unsuspecting victims. The pills can be either small, white and round or newer versions are oval and greenish-gray in color.

The newer pills have a dye that changes the color of the drink making them harder to slip to someone without their knowledge. These newer pills will turn a clear drink bright blue and dark drinks turn cloudy. However, in a dark drink or in a punch it will be difficult if not impossible to determine whether or not the drink has been compromised. This is especially true in a dark or dimly lit room or club. Since the round, white pills are still available, they represent the greatest threat as they are easily ground up into a powder and added to various liquids.

The effects of Rohypnol are experienced within about 30 minutes and may last for hours. To an observer you will look and act as if you are very drunk and exhibit behavior that is similar such as having trouble standing, slurred speech or passing out. Specific problems include loss of muscle control, nausea, dizziness, problems seeing, feeling sleepy or drunk (but without drinking much if at all), and in extreme cases—death.

The next is GHB—short for *gamma hydroxybutyric*. Some of the street names for this drug include Easy Lay, Energy Drink, G, G-juice, liquid X, Cherry Meth, Salt Water, Gook, Goop, Great Hormones, Grievous Bodily Harm (GBH as opposed to GHB), Gamma 10 and others. GHB comes in liquid form, pill form and powder form. If your drink has a slightly salty taste *(note one of the street names above is Salt Water for a reason)* it may indicate the presence of GHB. The salty taste can obviously be masked by mixing it with a sweet or fruity drink so that detection is difficult if not impossible.

GHB is *very* potent and acts quickly—a small amount can be felt in about 15 minutes but effects can last up to 4 hours. Because it is so potent, it is extremely dangerous and easy to cause an overdose in the victim. Similar effects as Rohypnol are felt, that is, drunk-like symptoms including a state of relaxation, drowsiness, dizziness, and nausea. However, additional and more severe effects may include seizures, tremors, difficulty breathing, sweating, and vomiting. Overdose can occur when the heartbeat slows to the point where the victim enters a coma and finally dies.

The third is Ketamine. This also goes by a wide variety of street names including Black Hole, Bump, Jet, K, Special K, Purple, Cat Valium, Green, K-Hole, Kit Kat, Super Acid and others. It is available in both liquid and white powder form.

Ketamine is extremely fast-acting and produces a variety of symptoms that are similar to those felt during an acid trip, hence one of the street names—Super Acid. The victim may be aware of what is happening but is powerless to prevent or stop it. It also causes memory problems, and so the victim may not recall exactly what happened, even if they were conscious when it was occurring. Various changes to sensory perception occur including distortions in sights and sounds, out-of-body experiences, loss of time, a feeling of being out of control and the loss of motor function. Victims may experience difficulty breathing, convulsions, vomiting, numbness, aggressive behavior, elevated blood pressure and memory problems.

In the 1990s, Ecstasy was a very popular party drug. It goes by several other names including MDMA, Molly, XTC, X, Love Drug, Adam and Clarity. It is a synthetic, psychoactive drug. As the name implies, ecstasy provides the user with positive feelings toward others, a general sense of well-being, decreased levels of anxiety and even enhanced sensory perception. The positive effects typically are felt within about an hour, but the negative effects can be felt for up to a week or longer, and may be severe.

Negative effects of MDMA use include anxiety, sadness, lack of appetite, thirst, reduced interest in sex and reduced pleasure from sex, and significant problems with mental function. Irritability and aggression are also experienced in many users after use.

From a health standpoint, users can experience chills, nausea, sweating, muscle cramps, blurred vision, dangerous rise in body temperature (hyperthermia), and various heart-related problems including irregular heartbeat, high blood pressure and even heart failure. Some of these symptoms are also seen in overdose situations which may also include panic attacks, loss of consciousness and seizures.

The body has difficulty processing and breaking down MDMA. If additional doses are taken, it can have rapid and severe health consequences as outlined above. In addition, it also interferes with the body's ability to break down other drugs which may be present in the body. The mental effects can be severe as well since the drug interferes with memory. This can cause problems with the brain's ability to process complex tasks or skilled activities which can directly affect things such as driving and schoolwork.

College is a stressful time—you have a lot of work to do for a variety of different classes and professors. You may also be working at a part-time or even a full-time job or simply overwhelmed by the sheer amount of things you have to do. If you believe or are told that taking some sort of drug can help ease your stress level or give you the energy you need, it becomes enticing.

Drugs such as *Adderall* (the "study drug") are stimulants typically taken in tablet or capsule form that helps keep students awake in order to get all their work done on a minimum amount of sleep. This can have long-term negative effects if used excessively because you are not giving your body the rest it needs in order to stay healthy. Increased use of *Adderall* and other stimulants is becoming a problem on college campuses around the country. Other stimulants include Ritalin, Concerta, Biphetamine, and Dexedrine. They go by the street names R-ball, Skippy, Vitamin R, Speed, Bennies, Black Beauties, Crosses, Hearts and Uppers.

Keep in mind that possession, manufacturing or delivery of any of these "party drugs" is a Class 3 felony in most states and you will be subject to 2–5 years in prison and a fine of up to $100,000. You think college is expensive now? How about tacking on another $100,000 and spending a few years of your life in jail? Federal law is even more severe depending upon the amount—and we're not talking large amounts either. For just 1 gram, you could be looking at 20 years in jail and a $1,000,000 fine!

Most users never consider these ramifications and you need to be aware of just how severe the punishment is for even possessing small amounts of these so-called "party drugs." If you have more than just a single pill or a single container, you most likely will be charged with possession with the intent to deliver. If you are found to distribute to someone under 21 (and most college students are under 21), the fines and prison time <u>double</u>. *If you are convicted, you will also lose any federal student aid benefits including loans, grants and work study.*

A popular illegal drug that is also a stimulant is cocaine. It also goes by a variety of street names such as coke, snow, blow, rock, flake, sugar, white horse and others. Highs from cocaine can last anywhere from 20 minutes to an hour or so. When you come down from the cocaine high, you typically want more and so do more and more. It is highly addictive! Do not do it! A good mantra to remember is, "Why snort something up your nose when you spend your whole life trying to blow stuff out?"

An extremely dangerous combination called a "speedball" is a mix of cocaine and heroin that is injected via needle directly into the bloodstream. They have opposite effects on the body since cocaine is an upper or stimulant and heroin is a downer or depressant. Stay far away from anything using a needle or that must be snorted or smoked!

Alcohol is by far the most popular drug on college campuses and yes, it is a drug. Due to the fact that drinking and college tend to go hand-in-hand, it is more acceptable than other drugs among students. However, it is no less dangerous when abused. It is addictive and may cause health problems. The effects of alcohol were already previously discussed in detail, so they won't be rehashed here.

Marijuana has become the next most popular drug in colleges across the country due in large part to the legalization of it. It is currently legal for recreational use in 7 states including the District of Columbia. In addition, medical marijuana is legal is 20 states plus the District of Columbia as of this writing. This does not make it any less of a problem for college students, however. On some campuses, the use of pot is even greater than alcohol consumption. It is still illegal under federal law, however.

Marijuana gives the user a "high" that varies by user. Some users are energized and want to get out and do activities—

typically in nature. Others get relaxed and want nothing more that to watch TV and feed the "munchies." Pot is an appetite stimulant which is why it is given to cancer patients that lose their appetite due to chemotherapy.

A marijuana high can last anywhere from 20 minutes to 2 hours or more depending upon the tolerance of the user and the strength of the "weed." *Unlike other drugs, there is no physical addiction to it.* Users may *want* to smoke, but they don't *need* to. This is a major difference between marijuana and other drugs. Many studies say that marijuana is a "gateway drug" meaning that if you try it you will want to try other drugs. Of course, if someone has tried marijuana—or alcohol or cigarettes for that matter, they are more likely to try other drugs.

Cigarettes are extremely addictive, yet they are legal. Cigarettes contain approximately 600 ingredients that when burned, create more than 7000 chemicals. Of these, 69 of these are known to cause cancer. This raises the obvious question—why would anyone begin to smoke cigarettes!?

If you currently smoke, you may need to rethink this very dangerous activity, especially after reading the following . . .

Many of the chemicals found in cigarettes are also found in a variety of other products. When they are, they contain a label warning the consumer and the general public that the product contains it. *However, although cigarettes contain a warning label, they do not list any of the specific ingredients found to cause cancer.* Some of the chemicals found in cigarette smoke include acetone (nail polish remover), ammonia (cleaner), arsenic (rat poison), butane (lighter fluid), carbon monoxide (car exhaust), formaldehyde (embalming fluid), lead (batteries), nicotine (insecticide) and tar (paving roads)!

Remember—any drug that affects your behavior or judgment can put you at risk. This includes alcohol and all of the above-described drugs. Although alcohol is by far the most common, you need to be aware of the other potential risks to your safety from these other drugs.

How do you protect yourself? Many of these drugs are difficult if not impossible to detect by taste, sight or smell once they are in a drink, so what can you do? The following three lists contain a) specific things to be aware of to keep you safe,

b) ways to determine if you may have been victimized and finally, c) what to do about it.

1. Don't accept drinks from other people—especially strangers. Even a bottle of beer that looks like it is closed could have had the cap twisted off, a date rape drug added, and then the cap twisted back on. *It is nearly impossible to discern whether or not a drink has been tampered with, so when it doubt, just politely refuse.*

2. Keep your drink with you at all times—yes, even when you go to the bathroom. You may be tempted to leave it with a friend, but how do you know that they will be holding onto it and watching it every second you are gone? Remember, it only takes a split second for one of these drugs to be slipped into a drink, so *keep your drink with you.*

3. *Refrain from sharing drinks.* You may have been watching your drink diligently all night, but what about your friend that wants you to try their drink? Again, politely refuse if you have any doubts as to the safety of <u>any</u> drink!

4. As stated earlier, one of the easiest ways to drug someone is by using a community punch bowl or large, open drink container. These concoctions may already have drugs mixed in, ready for unsuspecting victims to take a drink. *Your best bet is to pass.*

5. If someone at the bar or party offers to get you a drink, go with them and keep an eye on the drink at all times. It's great if someone wants to buy you a beer or mixed drink, *just watch it from the time it is opened or mixed until it's in your hands.*

6. As mentioned above, *if a drink tastes or smells funny, do not drink it.* GHB may have a salty taste, and most drinks should not taste salty! When in doubt, get another drink or stop drinking.

7. If at all possible, go out with a friend that isn't drinking. Of course, even the water they are drinking could be tainted with a drug, but this should at least lessen the chances of something happening to that person. If you start feeling strange and suspect you may be drugged, let that person know immediately and take appropriate action. *Leave the*

party and get to a hospital if you suspect you have been drugged.

8. *If you do end up leaving your drink unattended at a party or club and realize it, do not drink it.* <u>Pour it out</u> (it may be drugged and you don't want someone else drinking it!) and get another one. Don't take a chance.
9. If you begin to feel drunk and haven't had anything to drink, or only a very small amount, there is a good chance that you may have been drugged. Leave with a friend (not alone!) and have them get you to a hospital. *If you experience any of the above-described effects of these various date-rape drugs, seek immediate help.* Call 911 if necessary.

If you wake up or "come to" and don't remember what transpired the night before or from the past several hours, you may have been drugged and not remember it. You may be able to tell, but it may be difficult especially if you don't remember anything. There are three ways you might be able to determine if you were drugged.

1. If you wake up with a "super hangover" you may have been drugged. This could happen if you didn't drink much, or perhaps didn't drink at all. You may feel disoriented and confused and have a lapse in your memory where you cannot remember what transpired earlier in the evening or the night before.
2. Your clothes may be damaged, torn, missing or not fit on you properly—as if someone else put them back on you. This is a very disturbing thing to discover, but could be a clue that something happened without your knowledge or consent.
3. You may feel like you had sex but can't recall having it. You may feel sore or your privates may be swollen. If so, there is a very good possibility that you were the victim of a sexual assault / rape.

If you believe that you are the victim of rape or sexual assault, there are some steps to take that are *extremely important to the integrity of any police investigation* that need to be followed in order to <u>preserve evidence.</u>

1. As soon as you determine that you may have been drugged and possibly raped, secure your room and get to a hospital right away. Call 911 or have someone you trust take you. Do not attempt to "clean up" in any way. This includes washing your hands, brushing your teeth, or changing clothes (bring a change of clothes, however in case the police want yours as evidence). Try not to go to the bathroom, and definitely do not shower or take a bath. *It is imperative to follow these directions because the hospital will use a "rape kit" to collect evidence.*

2. Once you are at the hospital, unless the police were already dispatched from your 911 call, call them next. Be sure to tell them exactly what you remember, and what you cannot. *Do not leave out any details* that could help the investigation and <u>be honest</u>—even if that includes your telling them that you drank or did illegal drugs. *Even if you did, nothing "justifies" a rape.*

3. As discussed in the section above about the specific characteristics of date rape drugs, many of them leave your system rapidly. Be sure to have the hospital take a urine sample as soon as you can get them to. This is so that any potential traces of the drugs in your system are preserved as evidence. *This is the main reason why you should not urinate before getting to the hospital.* If you must, preserve your own urine sample by using an empty water bottle or something similar. The drug GHB is out of your system in 12 hours. Rohypnol can be detected in urine for up to 72 hours. However, you do not want to take a chance in missing out on a key piece of evidence—in fact, it could be the <u>only</u> piece of evidence.

4. With regard to where you woke up, whether it is your own apartment or home or somewhere else, *do not clean up anything.* If the assault occurred at the home or apartment of someone else, implore them not to touch anything until you tell them it's OK to do so. A forensics team will most likely want to go over the scene and try to pick up any other evidence such as fingerprints or bodily fluids. Leave the sheets on the bed and don't touch anything.

5. *Finally, there is the post-traumatic care.* You will most likely need to speak with a counselor or mental health

professional in order to help the healing process. You will experience a range or emotions including guilt, fear, shame, anger and disbelief. This is completely normal due to what has happened to you. You will have a hard time trusting people in the future, and may be afraid to explore an intimate relationship for quite some time. Talking to a professional and getting help is a very important part of taking your life back. There are many crises centers and hotlines that can help. You may want to call and speak with a professional anonymously over the phone. One resource is the *National Sexual Assault Hotline*—you can call them toll-free at 1–800–656–4673.

Additional resources include the DEA (www.usdoj.com/dea), www.MenCanStopRape.org, the *National Center for Victims of Crime* (www.ncvc.org) and the *Rape, Abuse and Incest National Network* (www.rainn.org).

Special thanks to the *Office on Women's Health* in the *Department of Health and Human Services* (www.womenshealth.gov) for providing much of the information and statistics in this chapter.

Part 5: Caffeine and Energy Drinks

Energy drinks often become a staple of the busy, overworked and stressed out college student. It can seem like each professor thinks that their class is the only one you have! They give so much work, but so do all your other professors. How in the world can you possibly get it all done? The answer for many college students is caffeinated energy drinks.

Over the past few years, an increasing number of energy drinks have appeared on the market. It used to be the realm of a handful of brands that became household names—*Red Bull, Monster* and *Rock Star* are a few that most people have heard of. Now there is *5 Hour Energy* and the various knock-offs that have come along after it. These super caffeinated drinks and potions promise to increase energy, eliminate drowsiness and heighten awareness. Drinks now include *Kickstart* and *Amp* (by *Mountain Dew*), *Bawls, Full Throttle, Jolt Cola, NOS, Venom* and many others.

The amount of caffeine in many of these beverages is startling. They range from around 80mg per serving for *Monster* (regular) to a whopping 300mg per serving in *Blue Charge* and *Bomb Energy Drink*. Keep in mind that many of these technically have more than one serving in each container. By drinking the entire bottle or can, you can be ingesting between 200—1200 mg of caffeine! By comparison, an 8oz cup of coffee contains between 50mg and 125 mg of caffeine. These drinks have directly contributed to a sharp rise in emergency room visits. From 2007 to 2011, the number basically doubled from around 10,000 to 21,000. Most of the cases were young adults between the ages of 18–25. The next group was 26–39. (http://www.webmd.com/hypertension-high-blood-pressure/news/20131202/energy-drinks-affect-heart-mri-scans-show#1)

For a complete listing of energy drinks, check out the *Wikipedia* entry for energy drinks at https://en.wikipedia.org/wiki/List_of_energy_drinks.

So does consuming a large amount of caffeine over time affect your health? You bet—in a BIG way. *First of all, caffeine is a drug.* In fact, it is the number one most used and abused drug in the world. It may not be exactly like some of the illegal drugs we have discussed to this point, but it can be just as dangerous. This section on energy drinks has been included to inform you as to the dangers of caffeine—the main drug in energy drinks.

Ingesting even relatively low amounts of caffeine over the long term causes caffeine to build up in your system. If you are drinking lots of caffeinated coffee, either huge "grandes" at your favorite *Starbucks* or your go-to energy drink, the effects are the same, and they are not good.

Most people know that caffeine increases heart rate which in turn increases blood pressure. However, long-term high blood pressure can contribute to heart disease and an increased chance for heart attacks and strokes. If you are over the age of 35, the risks are even greater. This is not to say that it is OK if you are under 35, but it is worse for you. Regardless of age, if there is a history of heart-related problems in your family, be careful. Caffeine also dehydrates the body, and so energy drinks should not be consumed when working out. The combination of fluid loss from sweating and the energy drink may cause dehydration.

Think you're stressed out now? Guess what? *Caffeine actually stimulates the production of stress hormones!* That can lead to even greater levels of stress, anxiety, and insomnia. Introducing additional caffeine into your system actually harms your ability to handle stress. Also, since caffeine increases the level of acidity in your blood, you end up with decreased immune system function. This can increase your chances of getting sick. You don't have time to get sick at college!

Your mood is affected when too much caffeine is present. You may feel more anxious and irritable and become more prone to panic attacks. When you come down and "crash" after the caffeine wears off, you may even feel depressed. You may require additional caffeine to feel "yourself" again. This is *withdrawal* that comes from reducing or eliminating your consumption of caffeine, and it is very real. Serious headaches, physical weakness and overall fatigue are all symptoms of caffeine withdrawal.

Many people are not aware that one of the other negative effects of caffeine is that it actually *decreases* blood flow to the brain by up to 30%. This has a negative effect on memory and mental performance! Think staying up all night studying with a few energy drinks will get you a good grade on that test? Think again! It may have the exact opposite effect!

When you think about diabetics and insulin shots, you probably don't equate that with your consumption of energy drinks. *However, caffeine stimulates blood sugar which causes your body to produce more insulin than it needs.* A short while later you may "crash" and feel tired. You may also get hungry and crave carbs and sugars. This is not good for anyone trying to get in shape, stay in shape, or diet! In addition, insulin tells the body to store fats and sugars. If you are an athlete in college, this can have a direct, negative effect on your physical performance.

Just like the increased potential for heart-related problems if they exist in your family, the same is true if you have any diabetes in your family. Increased, regular intake of caffeine will have a seriously negative affect on your body's insulin production. This will make you more prone to become diabetic. If you are already a diabetic, this will wreak havoc on your ability to regulate your insulin because your levels will continually spike up and down with your caffeine intake.

As if this wasn't enough to get you to swear off energy drinks—or at least, to curb how much you drink them, there is more. A host of problems can arise with your gastrointestinal system as a result. Caffeine's acidic nature can cause problems with your stomach including an increased risk of developing ulcers. It can also cause indigestion, heartburn and acid reflux over the short term, and can lead to stomach cancer over the long term.

There is more bad news. Caffeine actually prevents the absorption of some vitamins and minerals! This can lead to problems with your bones over time because the things you need for strong bones including calcium, magnesium, potassium and iron are no longer absorbed properly. Instead, they are passed out as waste. This is one major reason people develop osteoporosis as they age. The nutrients necessary for strong bones are no longer being absorbed by the body as they once were. If you drink a lot of coffee or caffeinated drinks, it is very important to replace those lost minerals. Take a good multi-vitamin, additional calcium and magnesium. They are essential to strong bones and joints. You should take a good, high-quality multi-vitamin that has a high rate of absorption. Don't take the cheapest one that may just pass right through you!

Men may worry about performance. The sheer number of ads on television for various male sexual performance enhancing drugs are a testament to that. However, did you know that caffeine also causes inflammation of the prostate and problems with frequent urination? An enlarged prostate is one of the main culprits of decreased sexual performance in men. Want to perform at your best and stop getting up at night to pee? Cut out the energy drinks and coffee!

Ladies, you have your own set of unique problems as do the men. Caffeine can cause additional problems with women who are taking birth control pills. These pills decrease the body's ability to process caffeine and a buildup can cause cysts in breast tissue. Caffeine also increases the risk of miscarriage and low birth weight babies. For older women, it can make menopause and hot flashes worse. The issues of osteoporosis discussed above are an even greater problem for women as they age, so reduce or eliminate your caffeine intake!

Have you been feeling tired and fatigued but don't know why? It could be the amount of caffeine you're taking in. Caffeine affects the body's adrenal glands which regulate stress and also produce anti-aging hormones. When we ingest caffeine, it does some of the work of our adrenal glands, and so they work less. The more tired we feel, the more caffeine we "think" we need, but the opposite is true! You need to cut out the caffeine in order to get your body's adrenal glands to do the job they were designed to do. They help you deal with stress—both physical and mental. Many negative health effects including irritability, anger, fatigue and the inability to get a solid, restful sleep are all negative consequences of caffeine consumption.

There are so many negatives with regard to caffeine, *here is one final one to think about.* We already discussed how caffeine causes your body to not absorb certain vitamins and minerals. In addition, it is also a diuretic which causes your body to lose water, meaning that your body will age faster as a result. Dehydration will cause many of your body's organs, including your body's largest organ, the skin, to age prematurely. The two most important internal organs are also affected—the liver and kidneys. If they cannot work effectively, they will be unable to process the toxins out of your body as they should. This causes toxins to build up in the body and inhibit the body's natural ability to repair itself. This causes premature aging of the body—both inside and out.

One last item of note—there are some alcoholic drinks that are mixed with energy drinks. This is a very dangerous combination because you end up with a wide-awake drunk. This person may not feel like they are drunk because of the stimulation of the caffeine in their system, but they still are. Unfortunately, people who consume these types of drinks are roughly 4 times as likely to drive a car because they "feel" sober when they are not. They still have the same blood alcohol content, and the risks are the same. Drinking and driving do not mix—with or without energy drinks!

Prescription Medication Abuse

The biggest problem with drugs in the United States is not on the streets in our towns and cities . . . it is in medicine cabinets in our bathrooms. Used properly under medical supervision, prescription medications are beneficial for those to whom they are prescribed. The problems begin when they are either abused or misused by the intended user. It is even worse when they are used by those who were not prescribed them at all.

The abuse of prescription medications has skyrocketed in recent years. Some of the most popularly abused are the pain-killers *Oxycontin* and *Vicodin*, sedatives *Valium* and *Xanax*, and stimulants *Adderall* and *Ritalin*. The myth that they are "safer" than other drugs is <u>completely wrong</u>.

There are serious legal problems that can occur if you are found in possession of or selling prescription medication. Depending on the drug, you may experience serious health problems as a result of using a medication that you are not meant to take. There is a reason for the prescription—they are designed to be issued by a licensed medical doctor and taken under their supervision. *Never self-diagnose or self-prescribe any medication.*

If you are taking prescription medication, keep it safe and secure—lock it up if necessary to prevent it from being stolen or abused. If you no longer require medication, then be sure to dispose of it properly so that it does not fall into the wrong hands. Do not be tempted to give it away or sell it to someone else. This is a serious crime with serious jail time and serious fines attached. For more information, visit http://go.osu.edu/generationrx

Chapter 7 Checklist: Alcohol Responsibility / Party Drugs / Prescription Abuse

✓ Both alcohol and illegal drugs (so-called "party drugs.") impair your judgment and ability to make proper decisions. You will forget things, become careless and lose inhibitions. Do so at your own risk!

✓ Excessive drinking is defined as 4 drinks at a time for women or 5 drinks at a time for men. Heavy drinking is defined at

8 or more drinks per week for women, or 15 or more drinks per week for men.

✓ 90% of rapes on college campuses involve alcohol and 73% of assailants and 55% of rape victims used alcohol or other drugs prior to the assault.

✓ Any sort of first-time drug use will have an unknown effect on you.

✓ College is a huge investment in your future; don't jeopardize it by making poor decisions as a result of drinking or doing drugs.

✓ Being highly intoxicated or drugged deadens your senses which could prove to be fatal in the event of a fire or other emergency.

✓ Alcohol poisoning can occur the very first time you drink. Many long-term health risks can also arise from excessive alcohol consumption.

✓ Approximately 30% of drivers who die between the ages of 21–24 had a blood alcohol level over the legal limit. Do not provide alcohol to minors!

✓ Never go out alone.

✓ Regulate your alcohol consumption.

✓ Don't accept drinks from other people.

✓ Never under *any* circumstances leave your drink unattended.

✓ Refrain from sharing drinks—you don't know if it was compromised.

✓ If a drink tastes or smells funny, do not drink it—especially if salty!

✓ All date rape drugs are powerful and fast-acting. Mixing them with alcohol makes them even *more* potent.

✓ If you are convicted of a drug-related offense, you will also lose any federal student aid benefits including loans, grants and work study.

Caffeine facts:

• Caffeine is the most used and abused drug in the world; watch your intake!

• Caffeine actually stimulates the production of stress hormones.

- Serious headaches, physical weakness and overall fatigue are all affects of caffeine withdrawal.
- Caffeine actually *decreases* blood flow to the brain by up to 30% which will have a negative effect on both memory and mental performance.
- Caffeine's acidic nature can cause problems with your stomach including an increased risk of developing ulcers.
- Caffeine actually prevents the absorption of some vitamins and minerals.
- Caffeine causes inflammation of the prostate which can lead to decreased sexual performance in men.
- Ladies, if you take birth control pills, know that these pills decrease the body's ability to process caffeine. A buildup of caffeine can cause cysts in breast tissue.
- Caffeine increases the risk of miscarriage and low birth weight babies.
- Caffeine can make menopause and hot flashes worse.
- Caffeine is also a diuretic and causes your body to lose water, which means that your body will age faster both inside and out as a result.

✓ There are serious legal problems that can occur if you are found in possession of or selling prescription medication.
✓ Never self-diagnose or self-prescribe any medication.
✓ If you are taking prescription medication, keep it safe and secure—lock it up if necessary to prevent it from being stolen or abused.

CHAPTER 8

Travel Safety—around Campus / at Home / Semester Abroad

No matter where you travel, either across campus or across the ocean, staying safe while you are going from place to place can be a challenge to your personal safety. Any time you are out in public or unfamiliar areas, you need to heighten your awareness.

Part 1: Traveling around Campus

When you first arrive at your new college, you will be dealing with a lot of moving around campus. Simply walking from place to place on campus may present safety challenges to you. A closed campus versus an open campus is one major difference. Depending upon where your campus is located is another. In addition, weather can cause a variety of safety concerns simply walking around campus when conditions become slick and slippery from rain, snow or ice. Allocate additional time to get to your destination. Don't wake up at the last minute and rush to class, only to find yourself lost and late. This will most certainly *not* make a good impression on your professors!

Take your time and learn the area so that you can feel comfortable with your campus and surrounding area. Look it up on maps (*Google Earth* or *Google Maps* is great for this!) and see what is around you. Check out naturally occurring land formations like rivers, forests and mountains. Also note where man-made structures such as major highways, shopping malls and apartment complexes are located. It is important to familiarize yourself with the area in which you now live. This way you know where both man-made as well as natural barriers exist that could be significant in case a natural disaster or act of terrorism occurs nearby.

Do not allow yourself to get complacent! Complacency leads you to *expect* things to be the *same* day after day. Most days this will be the case. However, don't be so naive as to think nothing will change and things will always be the same. A problem can and will happen to you or around you—it is not a matter of *if*, but of *when*. Stay vigilant and aware of the people, places and objects around you at all times. This way you can remain as safe as possible as you go about your daily schedule to classes, meals, the library, etc. Don't be paranoid, but be aware. If you are "armed with awareness™", it can never be taken from you and you will be ready when something happens. Be aware of what and who is around you as you walk around campus. Refrain from burying your face in your cell phone!

If you live on an enclosed campus, the threats from the outside will be limited. They will not be eliminated, only reduced to include your fellow students and teachers as well as outside guests and contractors. There is no such thing as being 100% safe—it does not exist. A fellow student may come to school one day and turn into an active shooter. A faculty member could be fired and return to campus to "settle the score" by deciding to hurt or injure anyone on campus. Outside guests and contractors are additional unknowns. You don't know who they are and what they are thinking. Contractors that work on campus hire and fire employees all the time. The person who was there for the last 3 months that you were familiar and comfortable with may be replaced by someone else today who maybe makes you feel uncomfortable. *You just don't know.*

If your campus is located in the middle of a city, the threats to your personal safety ratchet up a few notches. Outsiders who live, work or visit the city come and go all the time. They represent another set of people who you have to be conscious of. This should cause you to develop some additional safety habits that you need to practice anytime you visit *any* city in *any* state.

You won't be just walking around campus. Chances are you will also use some other form of transportation such as skateboards, ripsticks, scooters and bicycles which all present safety challenges. Keep your eyes in front of you and watch out for pedestrians and motor vehicle traffic. Not all drivers adhere to traffic signals, so do not assume that they will stop for a light or stop sign. There are many distracted drivers on the road—don't assume that a driver sees you crossing the street. Be alert so that you don't get hit by a car. Watch out for road hazards so that you don't get a wheel stuck in the sidewalk and go flying off your bike or board!

Of course, driving around a new area that you are not familiar with also presents a challenge. Take your time when driving in unfamiliar territory on streets that you don't know. It is easy to get lost or make a wrong turn and find yourself heading the wrong way. Use GPS to your advantage so that you can easily get back on track if you do take a wrong turn or find yourself lost.

Part 2: Semesters Abroad and Traveling to Foreign Countries

Traveling to another country presents another set of challenges to your safety and well-being. Things can get very complicated in a hurry. Dealing with another country's unique customs and traditions may not be the same as what you are used to in your home country.

Misunderstandings can and do occur—some may be innocuous, while others may be purposely hostile and represent a direct threat to your personal safety. Know the equivalent of 911 in any country you visit.

First, you must make sure that you have a valid passport and that you get any visas that you may need when traveling. Make copies of all travel documents including your passport and visas and keep them in a safe place apart from the original documents.

You need to be aware of any specific health challenges that could exist in the country you are visiting. Some may require that you receive special immunizations before you are allowed into the country. This means that you may be exposed to threats to your health that do not exist in your home country. If you take any medications and will be traveling with them, get a note from your doctor that says what the medicine is, the dosage, prescription duration, and what it is for. Keep this with you and with the medication at all times. Some medications may not be legal in the country you are visiting, so do the smart thing and plan ahead.

Another area you want to look into is health insurance coverage. Many domestic insurance plans cannot be used overseas, requiring you to purchase travel health insurance. Having it can be a literal life-saver in the event that you have to get medical treatment overseas. It can also help if you need to be medically evacuated back to the United States. The price for this coverage is modest, but could end up being essential if you need it.

The fantastic organization, On Call International sends nurses all over the world to assist US citizens in need of care or medical support while traveling. My own mother had this coverage while on a trip overseas in 2016, and needed to be medically evacuated to the United States. A fantastic nurse from On Call International (http://www.oncallinternational.com/; thanks, Lynne!) escorted her back to the US where I met them at the hospital. It was nerve-wracking, and my mom is OK now, but it was a scary ordeal. Plan ahead so that if you need coverage, get it! It is better to have it and not need it, than to need it and not have it. Learn how to say "help me" in the language.

Make sure that you research and read up on any type of travel restrictions that may exist where you are planning on going. You must be aware of any travel alerts or travel warnings related to the region or country you intend to visit. Your best bet is to check with the *US State Department* to see if there is anything that you should be aware of. You should also look up and get the contact information about the US Embassy or US Consulate in the country or region that you are visiting. For more information, visit http://travel.state.gov/content/passports/english/emergencies/crisis-support.html and also register with the Smart Traveler Enrollment Program (https://step.state.gov/step/) to get travel updates on your destination.

Another great travel resource can be found on the *Centers for Disease Control and Prevention's* web site at http://www.nc.cdc.gov/travel/page/survival-guide. The site covers everything from bug bites to traveling with animals to traveling while pregnant to water quality in foreign countries and much more. It is a site that you should visit before doing any travel outside your own country.

Dealing in a foreign currency also presents a challenge. The currency conversion can often be confusing, and so it is important to know exactly what it is since it can fluctu-ate day-to-day and month-to-month. What is a bargain today could cost double tomorrow. You will typically get the best exchange rate using your credit card, so it would be wise to have a credit card that you use solely when traveling abroad. Be sure to notify the credit card company in advance that any charges on that card during the time frame that you are going to be there are most likely valid and do not deny them! Keep an eye on your card at all times when paying for things so that no opportunity exists for the card information to be copied.

Keep a cheat sheet with you of the conversion rate as well as what you should expect to pay for your main staples in the coun-try you are visiting. Have this chart both in dollars as well as the foreign currency so that you know at a glance if something is fairly priced or over-priced. Spending a semester abroad is a long time to be in a foreign country. Be careful to plan accordingly for price differences where you are traveling to or you may end up running out of money before the end of the semester!

You may be used to paying $2.35 for a gallon of milk in the United States. That same gallon of milk would cost you about $4.00 in Canada or Russia. However, you could buy 3 gallons for the same $2.35 if you were going to India! A great barometer of cost-of-living expenses is to view the cost of *McDonald's* menu items around the world. Check out what a *Big Mac* costs around the world at https://www.statista.com/statistics/274326/big-mac-index-global-prices-for-a-big-mac/. This will give you a good idea of whether or not the country you are going to is cheap or expensive relative to the United States in US dollars. As an example, a *Big Mac* costs $6.35 in Switzerland, but only $1.46 in Egypt. That's quite a difference!

One area where prices vary wildly that may have a major impact on your travel plans is the price of gasoline. The United States pays one of the lowest prices per gallon of gasoline in the world. Countries that produce a lot of their own domestic oil and refine their own gasoline may have lower prices than the US such as Kuwait or Saudi Arabia. Conversely, countries that have to import most or all of their oil and gasoline pay steep prices.

A single gallon of regular unleaded gasoline in the US as of this writing is about $2.50/gal. In London you'll pay about

$4.50/gallon, in Hong Kong about $7.00/gal and in Germany about $10.00/gallon! You can quickly see how driving a car in other countries costs much more, and is the reason why many people in other countries drive smaller, gas efficient vehicles and not the huge gas-guzzling SUVs that many people in the US drive.

Keep in mind that other threats to your personal safety that you take for granted in the United States may not exist the same in other countries. One example is building standards related to fire safety. Do not assume that buildings in other countries have fire alarms, fire escapes or fire departments that are as capable as those you are used to. Some may be better, but some may be worse or non-existent. Become familiar with this aspect when traveling abroad and know your exits and evacuation routes.

Remember that you are more vulnerable when traveling outside your own home territory—wherever that may be. Once you leave your comfort zone and have to deal with new cultures and ways of doing things, you are at a distinct disadvantage to those who live and work in the area. Take time to learn local customs so you do not find yourself in an awkward or dangerous situation that may have been prevented if you understood what was going on more clearly. Visit the TSA web site (https://www.tsa.gov/) for additional information.

Chapter 8 Checklist: Travel Safety— around Campus / at Home / Semester Abroad

✓ Don't wake up at the last minute and rush to class, only to find yourself lost and late. Take your time and learn the area so that you can feel comfortable with your campus and surrounding area.

✓ Familiarize yourself with the area in which you now live so that you know where both man-made as well as natural barriers exist that could be significant in case a natural disaster or act of terrorism occurs.

✓ Be aware of what and who is around you as you walk around campus; refrain from burying your face in your cell phone! Do not allow yourself to get complacent, but be *armed with awareness*™ at all times.

✓ Keep your eyes in front of you and watch out for pedestrians and motor vehicle traffic. Not all drivers adhere to traffic signals, so do not assume that they will stop for a light or stop sign.

✓ Make copies of all travel documents including your passport and visas and keep them in a safe place separate from the original documents.

✓ Be aware of any specific health challenges that could exist in the country you are visiting. Some medications may not be legal in the country you are visiting, so plan ahead. Also learn the equivalent of 911.

✓ Research and read up on any type of travel restrictions that may exist where you are planning on going. Your best bet is to check with the US State Department to see if there is anything that you should be aware of.

✓ You will typically get the best exchange rate using your credit card, so it would be wise to have a credit card that you use solely when traveling abroad. Be sure to notify the credit card company in advance that any charges on that card during the time frame that you are going to be there are most likely valid and do not deny them!

✓ Remember that you are more vulnerable when traveling outside your own home territory—wherever that may be. Take time to learn local customs and ways of doing things so that you do not find yourself in an awkward or dangerous situation that could have been prevented if you understood more clearly. Learn how to say "help me" in the country's language.

Credit Card and ATM Safety Do's & Don'ts

Part 1: Credit Cards 101

On your journey from college student to responsible adult, a variety of financial challenges will befall you. Of course, there is how to pay for college for starters, but there are also daily financial challenges. Concerns such as having enough money to put gas in your car, pay for books, pizza, club dues, day trips, laundry, utilities or any number of things that cost money can be stressful.

The last thing you want is to incur more debt on top of your college loans. Additional, unmanageable debt in the form of high interest credit card debt is a huge mistake made by many college students. Some financial institutions come to college campuses and solicit students directly. Others simply mail credit card applications to you. There are also instances of fraud where criminals distribute fake credit card applications in order to get your personal information, so be careful!

The temptation of easy credit is a powerful one. You will undoubtedly be solicited heavily by various financial institutions to open a credit card account. Many will sound and look great on the surface, but initially low variable rate cards or ones that have zero interest for an introductory period often spike up to high levels after that period is over.

Discard any unused applications you receive by shredding them or disposing of them securely. This ensures they cannot be used by someone who fills them out and submits them on your behalf. A person could fill out the "pre-approved" credit card application using your info, but change the address to have the card sent to them! Now they have a card they can use and make purchases as you. This is easy for someone to do online, but not so easy off-line where ID is typically requested at the time the purchase is made.

Credit cards can be a valuable tool for controlling and managing your finances, but there is a right way and a wrong way to use them. Be sure to get all the facts and compare cards before committing to any. Ask your parents, teachers or your banker for assistance. They can be a valuable resource for you that could prevent you from making a big mistake.

Credit cards are the safest way to make online purchases. You can dispute charges made from a company if they misrepresent themselves. You are also able to easily dispute fraudulent charges if any are made on your card. In most cases your financial liability is limited to only $50. This is a lot better than losing out hundreds or thousands of dollars if you pay for an expensive item via check, cash or wire transfer. In addition, the balance is refunded to your card almost immediately provided you report the incident in a timely manner. Don't wait weeks to report a problem because it will be a lot harder to prove that there was an issue.

Some people feel that it is safer to *not* sign their credit card—this is a big mistake! If someone gets your card, all they need to do is sign your name with their handwriting, and it will match any merchant receipt that they also sign! Instead, sign the card and next to your signature on the credit/debit card, write "Photo ID Required." That way when someone looks at the signature to verify that it is signed, they should ask for photo ID. You can now *happily* provide it and show your ID to the person and thank them for asking! That is the whole reason for putting it on there. If the person does not ask you for ID, they are not doing their job properly.

Credit cards can be a useful tool, but carrying too many of them is not a good idea either. Having one or two cards with available credit is a good idea in case of an emergency if you need to make a purchase, rent a car, etc. In fact, some car rental companies will not take a debit card to secure the vehicle. Be sure to have and use a credit card for your car rentals. Typically you can pay when the car is returned with any form of payment, but you cannot use a debit card to rent the vehicle out.

Be sure to activate your new card as soon as you receive it and set your PIN *correctly*. That means not using obvious combinations of numbers like your date of birth, phone number, address or other easily discovered information about you. Pick some other relevant number that you can easily remember, or reverse the digits to make it even tougher. For example, if you met your spouse on June 7, 2012, instead of using "6712" reverse the number to be "2176." That way, even if someone tries a number that is relevant to you that they know, they still will not be able to easily guess it. You could go one step further and mix them up and make the PIN "1267." The point is to make a PIN that is easy to remember, but not easy to decipher!

Of course, don't write this PIN number anywhere—don't put it in your wallet, cell phone, car or anywhere else but your memory. Never give it to anyone. Banks and credit card companies will never call or email and ask you for it. If you receive a call or email asking for it, you know it is fraud and do not under any circumstances give it out. If you suspect your card is compromised, get a new card and set a new, different PIN. Yes, it can be a pain, but it is nowhere near the pain of losing hundreds or thousands of dollars from your account! When discarding your old or compromised card, be sure to cut it up and dispose of it properly. You can even go so far as to throw out part of your card in one trash can and the rest of it in another for additional security and safety.

When using your credit card for purchases, make sure that the amount you are agreeing to pay is what you are expecting and no more. Mistakes can happen just as easily as fraud, so it "pays" to "pay" attention (pun intended!) to what you are buying. This applies to both off-line, in-person transactions as well as on-line shopping purchases.

When using your card to make purchases online, make sure that the site is secure by showing a lock icon in the address bar. It should also start with "https" and not "http" to indicate a secure web site. It is highly recommended to use a credit card for online purchases instead of your debit card. That way if your card number is somehow compromised (such as the company's computer system is hacked), you will be able to easily dispute the charges and only be liable for $50. If your debit card linked to your checking account is used, it does not offer the same measure of protection, and may take much longer (if ever) to get your money back. Typically, you will be refunded, even with a debit card / checking account being compromised if it has the Visa or MasterCard logo. However, it may take longer which could impact your ability to continue to pay bills and have access to your money in order to live!

Another simple way to identify fraud is by monitoring your accounts online with your bank and credit card companies or by reviewing your printed statements when they arrive. If you do receive printed statements, secure them in a safe place or shred them after your review them. Most banks have online statements and online access to accounts, so it is very simple to keep an eye on your money. If you do not recognize a certain transaction or series of transactions, no matter how small, contact your bank or credit card company immediately. It may be a valid transaction run using a name that is different than what you expected, but it could also be fraud. Be on the lookout for several small transactions for amounts like $0.99, $1.00, $1.99, $5.00, etc. Often fraudsters will try a small amount to see if an account is valid before running a larger amount. Identifying the small charge before a large one occurs is important and can limit the damage done to your account.

Also be aware of emails that purport to be from your bank, credit card company or online retailer and warn you that your account is compromised. Follow up on those messages by calling their customer service number to ascertain whether or not the message is valid. *Do not under any circumstance reply to these emails directly, and certainly not with any personal information!* These are typically "phishing" scams that are mass emailed in the hope that some recipients will think it is real and click the link. This link typically goes to a web site that looks <u>very official</u> just like your bank, credit card company or retailer. However, that is where the similarity ends. It could be a site that has been set up for the sole purpose of defrauding unsuspecting account holders out of their hard-earned money. Do not fall victim to these scams! Some browsers and anti-malware programs detect these fraudulent websites and will alert you. They are not 100% accurate in detecting them, so always use common sense and err on the side of caution. Below are some examples of these types of emails.

> *"It has been detected that your collegename.edu email account has been infected with a virus. Your email account has is a threat to our database. You will need to update the settings on your collegename. edu email account by clicking on this link:*
> http://forms.bogusdomain.com/form/acct_update/1234"

> *"We suspect an unauthorized transaction on your bank account. To ensure that your bank account has not been compromised, please click the link below to confirm your identity and reset your password."*

> *"Urgent message. Our records indicate that over the past 24 hours your Amazon account may have been overcharged. Please sign in to immediately to verify that you did place any of these transactions. You must act within the next 48 hours to make sure the account receives the full refund."*

These messages usually sound ominous and tell you that you must act right away. If you have even the slightest doubt about the legitimacy of any messages that you receive, do <u>not</u> click the link in the message and do <u>not</u> call the number in it. Instead, log into your account as you normally would and as a precaution, you may want to change the password.

Note that some *key loggers* want you to do just that, and when you log in and change your password, the new one is actually *key logged* or captured and sent to the criminal. *Be sure that your system is clean of any viruses or malware before logging into any of your online accounts and updating your information.* It only takes a few minutes to update your software and run a full scan on your system, but the peace of mind and potential to thwart any scam is well worth the small inconvenience it may cause you.

Some companies will go so far as to actually call you on the phone in order to conduct their scam. Many people are tricked into providing enough information to the caller that completes their theft of your identity, your accounts and your money. The same safeguards must be adhered to when dealing with any unsolicited phone calls regarding a problem. Never give them any information including account numbers, PINs, addresses, middle names, social security numbers, etc. Politely tell the caller that you will call them back, and then look up the phone number for yourself—do not trust the number that they may provide to you.

If you think that your credit card or ATM card is lost or stolen, report it to the bank immediately. Every bank has a 24/7/365 phone number you can call to report a lost or stolen card. If any charges are put on the card after you report it stolen, you will not be liable for them at all. Should you locate the card after losing it, destroy it. You don't know if someone had access to it while it was "misplaced" so don't take any chances. Never leave your credit or debit card lying around your dorm room. Anyone entering your room could either take it, or simply take a picture of the card's front and back and now they have your credit card info. The same thing holds true for your bank statements—do not leave them lying around your room for prying eyes to see. You may trust your friends, but when tempted, even good people make bad decisions.

An excellent safeguard to protect your cards is to photocopy the front and back. Keep the copies in a safe or other secure location. In the event that your wallet or purse is stolen, you will know exactly what the cards were that you had. You will also have the phone numbers to call since those numbers are on the back of the cards. It is a small safeguard that can really simplify your efforts if it becomes necessary to cancel your card(s).

Finally, you must monitor your credit report from the main reporting agencies. You should be able to get a free copy of it every year from each of the three main ones—TransUnion, Experian, and Equifax. If you see anything on your report that you do not recognize, file a dispute with the agency immediately. You should be able to do this online by visiting http://www.AnnualCreditReport.com or the agency's web site directly.

Part 2: ATM Safety

Most people use ATM machines without spending a whole lot of time thinking about how safe they are. Using a well-lit ATM in the middle of a block is much preferred to using one on a

dark corner, for example. You want a good view of your surroundings before, during and after your transaction. There is
a lower chance of someone sneaking up on you and it is easier
to escape if necessary. Criminals who may be watching know
that you are almost certainly leaving the ATM with cash. This
makes you a prime target for thieves. If you feel uncomfortable
using an ATM, move on to the next one.

Know the location and be vigilant about observing everything around you that someone could hide behind. This
includes people, cars, buildings, landscaping around the area,
etc. Anything that blocks your view is a safety issue, so try to
use ATMs with nothing around them to obstruct your ability
to see on all sides. Even better, use an ATM that is close to
your school's security department or a highly trafficked area
such as your cafeteria or library. Bank ATM machines are typically under greater video surveillance, so they may be safer
than ones at a bar, mini-mart, gas station, shopping mall, or
restaurant. Using safer locations will help keep you safe and
prevent you from becoming a robbery victim—or worse.

Keep in mind that almost all ATM machines have a fish-eye
lens camera that can record a very wide angle. Be aware that
you are being filmed. Criminals may also know this, so they
will hold off on approaching you while you are near the ATM.
Once you are away from it and out of the camera's view, they
may make their move.

Before you even approach an ATM machine, you should
notice if there are people lingering around the area and not simply passing through. A car that is parked near an ATM with
someone in it may not be a patron . . . they may be a criminal looking for their next victim. Either wait a period of time to
see if they leave, or go to another ATM. It is better to be safe
than sorry! If something occurs while you are in the middle of a
transaction, the safest thing to do may be to cancel it and leave
immediately. If there is someone or something that just doesn't
seem right or feel right, chances are that there is a reason why
you feel that way. Trust your gut and your instincts!

There are many other considerations to be aware of when
using an ATM machine including using it for an after-hours
deposit. You want to have all the paperwork filled out ahead of

time so that you spend the least amount of time at the machine. The longer you are there, the more exposed you are and the greater the risk to your safety.

Use drive-up ATMs at all possible so you don't have to get out of your car. Make sure your doors are locked and all the windows are up except for yours and keep the car running. If something happens and you are approached, you can simply drive off. If your card is still in the machine, hit Cancel and grab it if you have time. If not, don't worry about it! The transaction will be canceled and you can get away safely. You can always get another card, but you can't get another you! Keep the music turned down and pay attention around you during the entire transaction.

Sometimes ATMs can act up and not work as expected. Be wary of anyone asking to help you with your transaction. Politely decline and move on to the next one. They may just be trying to help, but they may also be a criminal. If someone is nearby, position your body and hands in such a way that no one can see your PIN as you enter it, or the amount that you are going to withdraw.

When you do complete your transaction, don't stick around and don't count your money! Put it and the receipt away and check it when you are safely in your vehicle or other safe place. The chances of an ATM machine making a mistake is very, very remote, but even if it does you can't do anything about it by standing there yelling or cursing at the machine because it shorted you a $20! Get moving and deal with the bank later. You don't want to bring any attention to you, especially unwanted attention. (Side note: this is also true of any jewelry you might be wearing. Don't flash and flaunt it while you are out in public; it will attract attention, and all of it may not be good!)

If you discover that someone is following you after you leave an ATM, walk or drive as quickly as possible to the most public and crowded place you can. If you're in your car, drive to a police station or other heavily occupied public place. You can make noise to attract the attention of people who are there by flashing your lights, honking your car's horn, etc. Chances are the person following you will leave because they don't want to be the subject of all this extra attention and a lot of people who can give a description of them and their vehicle.

If this is not possible, and your greatest fear is realized and you find yourself the victim of a robbery, give them your money and any valuables they demand. You can always get another wallet, purse, credit cards, etc. Property is replaceable; people aren't. One thing you may consider doing is to throw your wallet or purse away from you. This will cause the thief to have to retrieve it. When they do, you can make your escape.

Skimming is a crime that you may not be familiar with. It uses a digital device such as a fake face plate to capture the data from an ATM or credit card transaction. They are commonly used on bank ATMs and gas station pumps, but they can be used just about anywhere credit or debit cards are accepted. The technology has evolved to the point where it has become very difficult to detect these devices because they are designed to match the equipment they are used on. They look like they belong there! If you observe something that doesn't look right such as a super thick credit card swipe or loose equipment connected to an ATM or credit card swipe machine, do not use it. There may be a skimming device attached!

If you suspect a skimming or "spoofing" device is attached to an ATM machine, gas station card reader or similar equipment, tug on the reader gently. This is a common practice in foreign countries, so when traveling, be particularly vigilant when using your credit or debit card.

A lower-tech version of this involves using a mirror and/or camera to watch you enter your PIN when you enter it. Then, the thief can rob you after you leave and use your ATM card to withdraw all your cash!

Be vigilant whenever you use your debit or credit card in public. Make the safest possible choices, and when in doubt, move on to another machine.

Chapter 9 Checklist: Credit Card and ATM Safety Do's & Don'ts

✓ Be wary of initially low variable rate cards or zero interest for an introductory period that may spike up to high levels after that period.

✓ Discard any unused applications you receive by shredding them or disposing of them in such a way that they cannot be used.

✓ Credit cards are the safest way to make online purchases.

✓ Having one or two cards with some credit on them in your wallet is a good idea in case of an emergency or if you need to rent a car.

✓ Activate your new card as soon as you receive it and set your PIN *correctly.* Do not using obvious combinations of numbers like your date of birth, phone number, address, etc.

✓ When discarding your old card, cut it up and dispose of it properly.

✓ When using your card online, be sure that the site is secure and has both a lock icon in the address bar as well as starts "https" and not "http."

✓ If you think that your credit card or ATM card is lost or has been stolen, report it to the bank immediately. Watch for skimming equipment.

✓ Photocopy the front and back of the cards and keep the copies in your safe or other secure location. That way you can cancel them quickly.

✓ Regularly monitor your credit report from the main reporting agencies.

✓ Use a well-lit ATM in the middle of a block, and try to use ATMs that are in plain view with nothing around them to obstruct your view.

✓ Notice if there are people lingering around the area and not simply passing through. Wait and see if they leave, and if not go to another ATM.

✓ For after-hours deposits, have all the paperwork filled out ahead of time so that you spend the least amount of time at the machine.

✓ Leave as soon as your transaction is complete—do not count money, etc.

CHAPTER 10

Dorm Room Safety— You & Your Valuables

Living on your own in a dorm will be a new and exciting experience. You may have a roommate, and living in a dorm means that you will be on a floor or in a building with other residents. You must be aware of a variety of safety concerns that could potentially befall you as a result of a problem in your dorm room or in another room in your building.

There are several safety concerns specific to living in a dorm room that you must familiarize yourself with if you want to ensure your safety. Threats can come from things that you or others do inadvertently as well as from threats done by others to you purposely.

Part 1: Fire Safety

First and foremost, <u>the most common and dangerous threat to your personal safety in your dorm comes from the threat of fire</u>. There are an average of 1800 fires that occur each year across the US in college dormitories, fraternity and sorority houses and off-campus apartments. This works out to around 5 fires a day at college campuses, but the number is most likely much higher since two-thirds of college students live off-campus and not all of those fires may be reported. According to Campus Firewatch (http://www.campus-firewatch.com/) newsletter, in the last three years, 52 students have died in fires at these residences. Each year in the US, more than 4000 people die in fires, and over 25000 are injured.

The need for awareness about fire safety is paramount for students off-campus more so than those on-campus. They do not have the support of campus resources including campus-monitored fire alarm systems and public safety officers to assist during a fire. If you are looking into off-campus housing, check to see if there are smoke alarms and sprinkler systems present. If not, you may want to look at another apartment. Your personal safety is too important to ignore just how important a *working* smoke alarm and sprinkler system can be.

Many dorms and student apartments are extremely susceptible to fire due to a lack of basic care and understanding about the dangers students are surrounded by. Most college students live in rooms full of clothes and papers strewn about, making the room a tinder box just waiting for a spark. That spark could come from overloaded electrical outlets and surge protectors, cooking, unattended candles or incense, and improperly extinguished cigarettes. These are some of the most common causes for fires among colleges. When you factor in that so many students live in close proximity to each other in dorms and apartment buildings, you can see that a very real problem exists.

Fire Facts:
(courtesy of http://www.campus-firewatch.com/)

- Fire is fast—in less than 30 seconds, a small flame can become a raging fire complete with thick smoke.
- Fire is dark—you cannot see fire once it begins burning in earnest because of the smoke it produces.
- Fire is hot—most people think of getting burned from a fire, but the heat generated can bring the temperature in a room up to 600°F or higher. At this temperature your lungs will be scorched by simply taking a breath. The heat can melt clothes to your body.
- Fire is deadly—the smoke and toxic gases produced by fires kill far more people than the actual flames do. Breathing these gases in can make you drowsy, short of breath and disoriented. If you pass out from breathing these fumes in, you won't wake up.

Some things you can do immediately to enhance your safety include the following:

- Keep your exits clutter-free so you have an unobstructed way out.
- Make sure that anything flammable is away from sources of heat and electricity.
- Don't store your bicycle, extra furniture, scooters or anything else in front of exit doors, halls and stairwells. This is a safety hazard for everyone in the building!
- Keep a list of emergency numbers including your campus public safety/security office, local fire, police and ambulance services in a highly visible location such as a bulletin board or on your refrigerator.

Having knowledge about the types of threats to your personal safety is a start. However, knowing that you have working fire alarms and how to quickly vacate your dorm or building is imperative. You may think about disabling a smoke alarm for any number of reasons, but think again. They are there for not just your protection, but the safety of everyone in the building or dorm you live in.

Do not cover them, hang things from them, remove or "borrow" their batteries or vandalize them in any way. Smoke alarms actually double your chances of surviving a fire. It is a crime to tamper with fire safety equipment and although it may be inconvenient to have to deal with a fire alarm from someone who burnt popcorn (again!), it is a small price to pay to learn how to efficiently and quickly vacate your room so you can stay safe at college—and that is what this book is all about.

In buildings with many apartments, a fire can quickly spread from one room or apartment to another. Fires double in volume every 30–60 seconds on average. Within a few minutes, an entire room will be involved. Never ignore a fire alarm thinking it is just another false alarm. It is better to be safe than sorry. If you are trapped because you didn't evacuate, you will be putting more lives at risk—the lives of the first responders. They will have to ignore their own personal safety in an attempt to rescue you. It may be a successful attempt, but it may not.

You should also be familiar with basic fire safety rules and guidelines.

- Make a step-by-step fire escape plan so you know how to leave any room. Each room should have 2 ways out—a primary and an alternate.
- Be sure that all your windows open so that if you need to get out, you can. (Of course, not if you're many floors up!)
- If you are on a 2nd or 3rd floor, it is a good idea to buy a collapsible ladder and keep it near the window in the bedroom.
- Keep a flashlight and whistle in every bedroom so you can see to get out and signal your location to rescuers if necessary. The whistle can also be used to alert others to a fire.
- Agree on a place to meet if you must evacuate your dorm or apartment so all roommates or tenants can meet up away from the building.
- Practice your plans so if you need to escape, you are prepared!

If you or someone else is on fire, here are some procedures to follow:

1. If you catch on fire, remember to STOP, DROP and ROLL until the fire is out. Rolling around on grass or dirt will take longer to put the fire out, but it will work. Run cool water over any burns.
2. If someone near you is on fire, and they are having trouble extinguishing the fire, you can help:
   a) get them to the ground immediately
   b) use a fire extinguisher if one is available
   c) cover them up with a (wet) blanket or towel in order to smother the fire (note: some blankets can melt, but the priority is to put them out, so use whatever is available as quickly as possible!)
   d) douse them with water if it is available (not for grease fires!)
   e) call 911 as soon as you can
   f) once the fire is out, attempt to remove the burned clothing, but not if it sticks to their skin
   g) keep burned clothing cool and wet
   h) wrap any exposed burns with a clean sheet

3. If you suspect that there is a fire on the other side of a door, use the BACK of your hand to detect heat and do not grab the handle. If the door handle is hot, do NOT open the door since you may cause a backdraft to occur. This will cause more rapid combustion and make the fire spread faster.

4. If the room you are in begins to fill with smoke, get down as low to the ground as possible and crawl out on your hands and knees. Smoke will rise and the cleanest air will be down low.

5. If you have access to water, douse an article of clothing, bandana, washcloth, towel, etc. with water and cover your nose and mouth in order to breathe through it and filter out some of the smoke.

Remember, these are general guidelines and not to be taken as medical advice. Consult with your doctor or other medical professional for more information.

Note: *Flashover* is a condition that occurs when the combustible gases from a fire rise in a room. They form an extremely hot layer of gas near the ceiling that can get up to 1500°F. This layer will continue to grow, move down toward the floor and heat up all objects in the room until everything in the room bursts into flame at once. This happens on average between four and ten minutes after the fire starts. This explosive force pushes the fire out into other rooms and grows hotter and hotter which makes the fire harder to extinguish. Once a fire gets to this point in a building or home, it is very difficult to save the structure.

Part 2: Electrical Safety

One of the best ways you can prevent a fire from starting in your dorm room is by being smart with how to deal with all your electrical appliances and electronic gadgets. It is very easy to run extension cords all over the place and plug in everything you have to available outlets. *This can be a big mistake.* Extension cords are designed as a temporary solution, not a permanent one. The longer they are, the more prone to failure they become over time.

Do not run them under carpets or put furniture on top of them. If they overheat or are damaged due to having heavy furniture placed on them, they can quickly overheat and start a fire. If you have the urge to string them up over doorways and around baseboards, be extremely careful and do not use staple guns to attach them to anything—inside or outside. The staples can damage the insulation that protects the wires and this can cause a fire as well. *Do not do anything that constricts, damages, bends or impacts the integrity of any electrical cord.* This goes for not just extension cords, but any power cord on any appliance or device. The smallest spark from a damaged cord can cause a fire if that spark happens to land on something that is highly flammable. Dorm rooms tend to be messy—there are probably clothes, papers, pizza boxes and other items in your room. If a spark lands on any of them, that could be all it takes.

Sometimes a problem can occur when you try to plug in a grounded (three-prong) plug into a non-grounded (two-prong) outlet. The biggest mistake you can make is to bend or cut off the ground prong and continue to use the device. This is a major safety hazard and creates a shock hazard. You have effectively disabled the ground which is designed to keep you safe. If you must, use a three-prong adapter plug. It contains either a ground wire or ground screw hole that you can attach to a two-prong outlet's face plate screw. This creates a proper ground that is not ideal, but does ground the device properly. It will help eliminate or reduce the potential for electrical shock. If you use the adapter and do not attach it properly, the problem will still exist.

Electrical sockets, cords and surge protectors can overheat, and when they do, they begin to deteriorate. If they are unable to function as designed, failures will occur in the form of shock, arcs or fire. Staying in an older building will increase the likelihood of this occurring. Older buildings were not designed to support the loads of today's electronic devices—especially all at once!

Use a surge protector that has over-current protection to minimize the risk of fire as well as damage to your devices. Also refrain from stringing multiple extension cords together as this can create an unsafe situation. It would be a shame to have your new smartphone damaged because you had it plugged into a power strip with too many other things!

Without getting too technical with regard to electronic ratings, know what your devices need and then add that amount up to see if what you are plugging them into can safely support it. If you are using an extension cord that has low-gauge wire (thin wire) that is rated for 325 watts, this means that the cord cannot safely support more. If you are using a surge protector that is plugged into that cord, but the surge protector is rated to support 750 watts, you CANNOT safely plug in more than what the minimum rated cord in the chain can support—in this case, 325 watts. This is very important for you to understand and will help prevent you from overloading your circuits in your dorm or apartment.

Most devices list their voltage and their amperage. Some may also list wattage. If they do not list wattage, simply multiply voltage x amperage to get the wattage. For example, if you have a laptop power supply that lists its output at 19 volts at 4.74 amps, when you multiply them together you get 90 watts. Know the wattage for all your connected devices and add them up so you don't create an overload condition. This is a key calculation if you are using a UPS (Uninterruptible Power Source) or battery backup. *If you exceed the rating of the UPS or surge protector, you will not get the protection you expect.* Take a few minutes to do some simple calculations and know that you are being as careful as possible.

It is normal for your power adapters and cords to get warm when they are charging or in use. Your outlets or devices should not get hot to the point where you cannot touch them without fear of getting burned. This indicates there may be a problem and a potential fire hazard. Immediately unplug some of the devices and place them on something non-flammable until they cool off. If you are within the rating of your cords or surge protectors, contact your Resident Assistant if you are on campus or your landlord if you live off-campus to address the problem.

A simple mistake that can also increase the risk of fire is the use of high wattage bulbs used in light fixtures or lamps not designed for them. This poses an immediate risk due to overheating, so be sure that you use only bulbs that are equal to or below the maximum wattage rating of lamps.

If you have washers and dryers in your dorm or apartment, be sure that their electrical cords are not obstructed or pinched. Also be sure to clear out the lint trap on the dryer before and after every use to prevent the buildup of lint which can also cause fires. *Clothes dryers cause hundreds of injuries and many deaths each year.*

Part 3: Cooking Safety

More fire alarms have been activated inadvertently as the result of cooking incidents than from any other cause. From burnt popcorn to microwave mac-n-cheese, cooking by college students is responsible for real fires almost as much as it is false alarms. *Cooking incidents are the second leading cause of fires in college and a leading cause of fire injuries.*

Many of these incidents could have been prevented if the person cooking simply paid attention and stayed in the kitchen! Distractions from the TV, cell phone, friends, etc. can take your focus off your task at hand. If your room begins to fill with smoke and the fire alarm goes off, your entire dorm or apartment building will have to evacuate. If it happens in the middle of the night, you can be sure there will be a lot of unhappy people!

Be sure that nothing flammable is near where you are cooking such as papers, curtains, clothing, towels, flammable liquids and cleaners. These all increase the risk of fire, so keep them all far away from your cooking endeavors. To help reduce the risk of fire, keep your cooking surfaces and surrounding areas clean and free of prior cooking adventures. This includes miscellaneous food particles, crumbs and grease.

Grease is especially dangerous because if it catches fire it cannot be put out with water—never throw water on a grease fire! Doing so can make the fire spread and catch more things on fire. The best way to extinguish it is to turn off the stove if possible, then cover it in order to starve it of oxygen. Once it is out, turn off the stove if you have not already done so.

Microwaves, toaster ovens, electric griddles, quesadilla makers and other cooking appliances are convenient items for cooking at college. Each one carries the risk of injury from burns and fires. Most microwave-related burns occur because the person removing the item that has been microwaved isn't aware of how hot the food is. Simply stirring microwaveable foods distributes the heat more evenly which can help prevent burns. Waiting at least 1–2 minutes after cooking has completed will also help prevent injury. Anything filled with liquids or jellies will also get extremely hot on the inside even though the outside may feel cool.

If you or someone near you gets burned, immediately place the burned area in cool water—do not use very cold water or ice. Cool water will ease the pain from the burn most effectively and prevent it from getting worse.

Keep a fire extinguisher handy. All dorms and off-campus apartments should have at least one fire extinguisher in them—preferably near the kitchen. Check that it has been recently inspected and that the needle on the gauge points to the green area. Read the instructions and familiarize yourself on how to use it. You don't want to be reading and learning how to use it when you need to put out a fire!

Drinking alcohol can also increase the risk of fire. You more susceptible to making a mistake or forgetting about something you put on the stove. You also won't wake up as easily if you are passed out drunk and not sleeping normally. Passing out or falling asleep in bed while smoking is a major cause of house or apartment fires. It is a sobering fact that approximately half of all adults who have died in house fires had high blood alcohol levels according to a study done by the US Department of Health and Human Services (https://www.hhs.gov/).

Any open flame or burning done in the confines of a home or apartment is a risk. Candles and incense cause approximately 12,000 fires per year according to the National Fire Prevention Association (NFPA). Many people leave candles burning unattended, yet every single candle comes with a warning label telling users not to! Just like when cooking, keep open flames from candles away from any sort of flammable material. Putting a candle on the kitchen counter may be nice, but an open window that blows the curtains over the flame may be a "recipe" for disaster (forgive the pun!) Of course, never empty smoldering ashes or hot wax into the garbage can or other container that may have flammables in it.

Don't assume that the fire alarms in your dorm or apartment are in working order; test them if possible. You always want to react as quickly as possible when you hear a fire alarm. You will likely deal with many false alarms in your college career as students inadvertently set them off. It is imperative that you refrain from becoming complacent and never ignore fire alarms. You may be tempted to do so, especially at an inconvenient hour like 3:00am, but chances are that the one time you decide to ignore it, there is an actual fire.

Once a fire alarm goes off, immediately stop what you are doing and exit the fastest way possible, closing your door behind you. Closed doors are barriers that can keep a fire from spreading. They may not stop a fire, but can slow it down. Do not use the building's elevators if they have them. Continue to exit your building as quickly and orderly as possible. *There is no reason to panic.* You should have had prior fire drills that have prepared you for a fire alarm in your dorm or apartment building.

However, a fire alarm could go off in one of the other buildings on campus that you have *not* had any drills in. *It is always a good idea to familiarize yourself with the location of any emergency exits and fire escapes.* If there are posted fire evacuation plans in the building, take a minute to read them. Even better, take a picture of them with your cell phone's camera so that you have them with you all the time. Do this for all the buildings on campus and you will be much better prepared than the majority of students. This will also enable you to assist your fellow classmates if there is a need to rapidly evacuate the building; the threat doesn't have to be just from fire!

Any time you enter an unfamiliar building, either on campus or off campus, it is a good idea to identify the ways in and out of that building. It could be a retail store, convenience store, restaurant, etc. Every building will have at least two entrances/ exits. If you cannot see the second one, chances are it is in the back where deliveries are made, or an employee entrance. If you need to quickly escape from any building, know at least two ways in and out. There is a good chance that the primary one will be blocked or inaccessible if the masses rush to it, or if a threat blocks it.

Something else to consider; you may not be able to see clearly if the building is full of smoke. *You should make note of where the nearest exit is and any distinguishing way you could locate it if it can't be seen.* Another way would be to count the doors from your room to the fire escape. This will save valuable time if you are trying to leave quickly but are having trouble seeing your way out. Remember to check any door handles using the *back* of your hand and do not open a door that is hot to the touch! Chances are there is a fire on the other side of the door, and if you open it, the rapid introduction of additional oxygen will cause a backdraft to occur. This will cause the fire to abruptly increase in intensity, potentially blowing back at you and injuring you.

If you notice yellow or brown smoke, lots of soot in the air, or small puffs of air coming from holes or cracks in a wall, door or window, watch out! There is a very good chance that a dangerous backdraft will occur if additional oxygen is added to the room by opening a door or window, so be careful and aware of these signs.

Always make sure you and your roommates are safe before worrying about any of your belongings or valuables. Things can be replaced; you cannot. If a small fire can be brought under control with a fire extinguisher and common sense, then by all means do so. *Be sure to keep your back to an exit and the fire in front of you.* That way, if you need to escape, the fire will not block your retreat. If you are unsure about how to fight a fire or use an extinguisher, then get out, call 911, and let the professionals deal with it.

A great resource that includes a checklist of questions to ask your college officials can be found at www.CampusFireSafety .org.

Part 4: Outside Threats

You want to believe that the people who live in your apartment, on your floor or in your building are good people. Chances are the vast majority of them are. However, you should still take basic security precautions with regard to securing your room and your valuables. The safety habits you hopefully grew up with should follow you to college. This includes things like not opening the door for strangers, even if you think they are students. If you don't know them, you are not required to open the door if you are uncomfortable.

It should be obvious, but lock your door every time you leave. This includes when you leave to check on your laundry or to see if a friend is around. It only takes a few seconds for someone to enter your room and swipe something of value. Laptop computers, cell phones, money, food or other items of value can be taken in the blink of an eye. Imagine your dismay to return to your unlocked room and find your laptop gone! The paper you were working on is gone too since it was on your laptop, along with your notes and other documents, pictures and videos.

Never give anyone your key or a copy of it. If you lose it or suspect it has been stolen, have the locks on your room changed immediately. Don't leave the door unlocked for your roommate if you aren't there or if you are going to sleep. Be sure they have their key and don't let them compromise your safety because they don't want the "hassle" of carrying their key.

In addition to locking your door, don't forget about your windows. This is especially pertinent if you live on the ground floor of a dorm or apartment.

There will be times when you are in your room but will not be able to keep an eye on everything. You could be sleeping or taking a shower with valuable items all around your room. Any of them could be removed without your knowledge. For this reason it is important to lock your valuables up both when you are out of the room as well as when you are in your room but unable to watch them.

One of the best solutions is to have a locking filing cabinet or desk drawers that you can secure your wallet, ID, credit and debit cards, checkbook, laptop, iPod, jewelry and other items of value in. Take it a step further and use a cable lock to secure that cabinet or desk to another piece of furniture like your bed. This will make it basically impossible for someone to steal your valuables because not only are they locked up, they are in a cabinet that is secured to another piece of furniture. You will gain tremendous peace of mind knowing that your valuables cannot be stolen . . . *just don't forget to lock them up!*

Any type of electronic valuable should be locked up using some sort of cable lock system. This holds true for computers, gaming consoles, televisions, printers, etc. Any valuable item you don't want to have stolen should be locked up with either a cable lock, or inside a locked safe or drawer when not in use. The items that are the most critical to keep secure involve those that contain your personal data—computers and cell phones. These have your emails, photos, account information and other data that could be exploited and used for identity theft or financial theft.

Although it should be obvious, never give anyone the combination to your safe or the key. Combinations can be shared, and keys can be copied.

A line of safes called *diversion safes* can work extremely well in a college environment. These are safes that look like everyday items or objects, but have compartments that can hide smaller valuables. Diversion safes include books, bleach bottles, salt containers, hair spray, soda cans, clocks, and fake surge protectors. They hide valuables in plain sight that the majority of people would never know are there. There are many other types to choose from.

Another good idea is to position your bed inside your room so that you can see the door while lying down. This will allow you to see if someone enters your room without having to get up or turn around first. This can save valuable time if something happens that requires you to act fast.

Keep a good quality flashlight near your bed that has a high lumen value and a strobe function. This combination will not only allow you to see who is there, but can blind them and disorient them with the strobe function. Small, compact flashlights can include these features and be extremely powerful. Larger flashlights can also double as a bludgeon weapon to defend yourself in a worst-case scenario.

If you have items that cannot be locked up due to their size or because of some other reason that makes it impractical, you can label the items. Use either a permanent label that contains your contact information or a more clandestine method such as an ultraviolet (UV) pen. This cannot be seen unless ultraviolet light is used to detect it. Having any sort of identifier on your valuables will make it easier for campus security or law enforcement to return your property if it is ever stolen. You should also take it a step further and take pictures of your valuables. Note the serial numbers of any valuables that have them. *Keep this information separate from your valuables so that it isn't stolen along with the items!* It is a good idea to keep that information at home, in a safety deposit box or similar secure location.

Having an inexpensive alarm that you can put on your door such as a wedge shaped door stop alarm can give you additional security. These alarms are basically just door stops that you place against the door. When the door opens, the alarm goes off. They can be purchased for under $5. Similar alarms can be inexpensively purchased for windows as well. These utilize a magnetic switch that when the window is opened past the connection, the alarm is tripped. You can buy a 4-pack for under $30 and they install in minutes.

Something that many parents and college students don't think about is getting insurance for valuables. *High value items such as jewelry, laptops, musical instruments, designer clothing and other items should be insured before taking them to college.* It is easy to get a supplemental insurance policy or rider to an existing policy that will cover these items for peace of mind. If you are living in off-campus housing, you may be required to have renter's insurance anyway. While you're at it, review your auto insurance policy and see if you have the proper coverage. You may need to adjust the amounts or change the policy to reflect that your car may now be used just for commuting. This could lower your automobile insurance cost. If your vehicle will be spending more time out-of-state than in your home state, you may need to register the vehicle there and get new plates.

If you have a vehicle, don't leave your valuables inside for all to see! Keeping your backpack in the rear seat, or your laptop case on the floor or seat is a sure-fire way to have your car broken into. If you must keep them in your car, lock them in the trunk or glove compartment and out of sight. If you have a hatchback, at least cover the objects with a blanket or clothing so that they are not in plain view. The best thing is to take them with you and not leave high-value items in your vehicle unattended.

Many college dorms have laundry facilities. If your building does, or if you go off-campus to do it, bring some homework or reading with you. Stay with your laundry while it is being done. Having some nice jeans or expensive shirts stolen out of your laundry would be a big loss. Many items of clothing are expensive. On a college budget, going clothes shopping is probably not near the top of your list!

The safety and security of your dorm or apartment is also an important concern. Does your dorm have security officers at the front desk? Are all guests signed in and out using a log book? Are there times when the desk isn't staffed? Is your building only accessible by key or swipe card? These are all valid concerns that contribute to the safety of your dorm or the lack of it. Knowing that procedures are in place to keep your building as safe as possible from outsiders and guests will give you additional peace of mind.

Most colleges use some form of student ID card. As technology is used with greater frequency on college campuses, these ID cards typically have magnetic strips like credit cards. They are swiped at card readers to gain access to various buildings on campus. Depending upon the complexity and programming capability of these devices, student ID cards may be programmed to only allow access to the building you live in and the buildings you have classes in. This is the best type of security because all swipes are logged in a computer. These logs can be audited if something occurs in a building. There will be a record of everyone who entered . . . or at least all those IDs that were used to enter the building.

Another point to remember is the concept of "piggybacking." This is when one student uses their ID to swipe in and gain access to a building, classroom or dorm, but one or more other students also enter the building. They "piggyback" on that person's card swipe instead of using their own. This may not be so bad when one student follows another student into a building, but what if a non-student enters a building they should not be in? They may have other plans such as stealing equipment or perhaps sexually assaulting someone in a dorm or apartment. *Always pay attention when entering a restricted area and don't allow others to "piggyback" on your swipe.* It is for your own protection as well as others on campus.

This brings up my next point—*never* lend your ID to another student or guest! If the person using it does something they are not supposed to, the records will show that you were there, even if you were not. If you tell investigators that you lent your ID to someone else, they may or may not believe you. Even if they do, you are sure to get in trouble for lending someone else your ID. You wouldn't lend someone your credit card, would you? *Then don't lend someone your student ID!*

Student ID cards are often used to pay for meals or to make purchases at the campus bookstore. The cards contain a record of the balance in the student's account. Someone else using your card could spend money on food or expensive college attire at the bookstore. You wouldn't know about it until you realized that you have less money than should. You may or may not be able to pull up a record of purchases made with your card. Keep your student ID with you at all times and protect it like a credit card or driver's license. If you lose it, report it to your campus security department immediately. They can issue you a temporary card until you either find your original or determine that it is gone for good. If it is, then they can deactivate it so that it cannot be used by anyone who has it.

Chapter 10 Checklist: Dorm Room Security—Keeping You & Your Valuables Safe

✓ The most common and dangerous threat to your personal safety in your dorm comes from the threat of fire. In the last three years, 52 students have died in fires at these residences.

✓ If you are looking into off-campus housing, check to see if there are smoke alarms and sprinkler systems present.

✓ Keep your exits clear of clutter so that you have an unobstructed way out.

✓ Smoke alarms actually double your chances of surviving a fire, so make sure they are working and do not tamper with them in any way.

✓ Fires double in volume every 30–60 seconds on average so within a few minutes, an entire room will be involved.

✓ Extension cords are designed as a temporary, not a permanent solution.

✓ Do not run extension cords under carpets or put furniture on top of them.

✓ Do not do anything that constricts, damages, bends or impacts the integrity of any electrical cord.

✓ Do not bend or cut off the ground prong on a grounded (3-prong) plug to make it fit into a non-grounded (2-prong) outlet. This creates a shock hazard since you have effectively disabled the ground which is designed to keep you safe.

✓ Use a surge protector that has over-current protection to minimize the risk of fire as well as damage to your devices.

✓ The risk of fire increases if you use high wattage bulbs in light fixtures or lamps not designed for them.

✓ Cooking incidents are the second leading cause of fires in college and leading cause of fire injuries.

✓ Grease is especially dangerous because if it catches fire it cannot be put out with water—never throw water on a grease fire!

✓ Keep a fire extinguisher handy, check that it has been recently inspected and that the needle on the gauge points to the green area.

✓ Candles and incense cause approximately 12,000 fires per year according to the *National Fire Prevention Association* (NFPA).

✓ Closed doors are barriers that can keep a fire from spreading. They may not stop a fire, but can slow it down.

✓ Any time you enter an unfamiliar building, either on campus or off campus, it is a good idea to identify the ways in and out of that building.

✓ Remember to check any door handles using the *back* of your hand and do not open a door that is hot to the touch! If you open it, the rapid introduction of additional oxygen will cause a backdraft to occur.

✓ Make sure you and your roommates are safe before worrying about any of your belongings or valuables. They can be replaced; you cannot.

✓ Be sure to keep your back to an exit and the fire in front of you.

✓ Be sure to lock your door every time you leave your room or apartment—even if for just a few minutes. It only takes a few seconds for someone to walk in and take something of value such as your cell phone or laptop.

✓ Have something like a locking filing cabinet or desk drawers that you can secure your valuables in.

✓ *Diversion safes* can work extremely well in a college environment. They look like everyday items or objects, but have compartments that can hide smaller valuables.

✓ For larger items, you can label them either with a permanent label that contains your contact information or use a more clandestine method such as an ultraviolet (UV) identifier.

✓ Take pictures of your valuables and also note the serial numbers of any valuables that have them.

✓ Do not allow others to "piggyback" on your swipe.

CHAPTER 11

Personal Safety Alarms and Apps

The rise in violence on college campuses has given rise to a new type of alarm—the personal safety alarm. Several manufacturers have created small devices designed to be used when your personal safety may be threatened. *They are intended to shock, disorientate, and scare off an attacker.* These devices can be held or worn, are relatively inexpensive and can be programmed to send the user's GPS location, audio and video to a set of contacts when a button on the device is pressed. This is an incredible innovation using the latest technologies. They allow a person to run away and escape as well as summon help to them immediately.

Personal safety alarms can be utilized anywhere—in your dorm or apartment, while out on campus and even while driving. They are an excellent deterrent since they can emit sounds up to around 130dB. This is loud enough to be heard from a long way away and alert anyone within range of a problem. To give you an idea of how loud 130dB is, it is comparable to you hearing a jet take off from 50 feet away. It is louder than a jack hammer, alarm clock, standing next to a car horn and a rock concert. The threshold of pain as a result of sound decibel levels begins at around 110db—120dB is painful. At 150dB your eardrums will rupture. At 194dB, sound waves become shock waves.

These personal safety alarms are excellent devices for anyone when out walking, running, hiking or engaging in any type of outdoor activity. They can be carried or worn and used when walking across campus or walking across town. They are a very effective deterrent at warding off aggressive attacks. Some of these alarms have a pin that is pulled out that activates the alarm like a grenade. The pin can be attached to your clothing, key chain, purse or something else so that when it is pulled out the alarm is activated and will stay active for up to a half-hour is some cases. If a thief grabs your purse, the alarm will go off and the thief will usually drop the purse and run. They are less prone to accidental activation than devices with a button. This makes them ideal for carrying places where you may want to ensure that does not happen such as classrooms and theaters.

They are relatively inexpensive, with most priced under $20. At this price, you can purchase several and keep one in your purse, one in your car, and one in your dorm room. They are small and easy to carry or wear. Some resemble a car remote which makes them inconspicuous and not easily detectable to attackers. There are models that include a small LED light so you can more easily find keyholes in the dark. There are many to choose from, so do your research and determine what features are important to you before deciding. The links in this section are a start.

Physical devices are a great help, but there is a way you can take it to the next level thanks to technology. You can use an existing device that you have with you most of the time (your cell phone) for personal safety apps.

These programs are set up in much the same way as physical devices, but are activated when the user presses a button on the phone or on the phone's screen. This allows you to easily activate the alarm without having to swipe your unlock pattern or enter your PIN first. Some even are activated when you shake the phone.

When activated, they can send out details about the victim's location and turn on the phone's camera and microphone. The captured audio and video can be sent to a programmed list of contacts. Some send a stream of data while others send information every few minutes to your contacts.

Another feature that some of these apps is a "buddy" function that allows you to monitor the location and status of a friend in real time. This can be very helpful if you want to monitor the progress of a friend as they walk or drive home.

Many college campuses have begun distributing personal safety alarms to incoming college students at no additional charge to the student. It is a small measure that can yield big results in terms of keeping the students of a particular campus secure. They may have links to the college's public safety department that tell the dispatcher who activated the alarm and where they are located. This assists public safety officers in finding the victim as rapidly as possible and rendering assistance.

The following websites contain additional information for your review.

---

http://www.protection1.com/campus-safety/student-safety-apps/#
.Vee9DZeHd8E

http://www.elle.com/culture/tech/news/a14941/womens-safety
-apps/

http://www.hongkiat.com/blog/android-personal-safety-women
-apps/

Chapter 11 Checklist: Personal Safety Alarms and Apps

✓ Personal Safety Alarms are intended to shock, disorientate, and scare off an attacker.

✓ They are a very effective deterrent at warding off aggressive attacks.

✓ Personal safety alarms can be utilized anywhere—in your dorm or apartment, while out on campus and even while driving.

✓ They can be carried and used when walking across campus or walking across town.

✓ They are relatively inexpensive with most being under $20.

✓ You can use an existing device that you have with you most of the time (your cell phone) for personal safety apps.

✓ Some of these apps have a "buddy" function that allows you to monitor the location and status of a friend in real time.

✓ When activated, they turn on the phone's camera and microphone to capture and send audio and video to a programmed list of contacts.

CHAPTER 12

Physical Threat Self-Defense / Safe Dating / Sexual Harassment / Rape Prevention / Tolerance

Part 1: Physical Threat Self-Defense

When a situation progresses beyond a certain point and someone "crosses the line" or your personal boundary (see Chapter 2), it may become necessary to defend yourself. *Threats of physical harm or sexual assault demand a decisive and immediate response.* You must make sure that you know this and are mentally and physically prepared <u>before the need arises</u>.

Taking self-defense classes is a good start if you have the time and the money. When you're in college, you probably won't have either!

That's OK, because there are some simple self-defense principles that anyone can quickly learn. You might think that you have to train multiple days a week for years in order to become proficient at defending yourself. *This is simply not the case.* As someone who has taught a wide variety of people of all ages, sizes and shapes, I can tell you that <u>anyone</u> can learn to effectively defend themselves against a larger, stronger attacker. They simply must learn a few basic principles and how to apply them.

There are two purposes of this section. The first is to provide you with information that can help you prevent a situation from escalating to a physical confrontation by recognizing what is happening. The second is to be able to decisively end an attack with brutal effectiveness if necessary.

Some of the concepts you have hopefully already learned from previous chapters such as being "armed with awareness™" at all times in all places.

First, being aware of the people around you at all times is imperative. Anyone could be a potential attacker, but that doesn't mean that you should view everyone as an immediate threat. It simply means that you must notice things that warrant additional attention. If you see something that gives you a reason to be suspicious, don't ignore it! Someone who looks out of place either by the way they are acting or by what they are wearing or doing should be a signal to you. Keep an eye on them or even vacate the area and alert someone to your suspicions.

Second, the environment you are in plays a large role in your personal safety. If you are in an unfamiliar building such as a restaurant, store, or club that you are at for the first time, you are already at an immediate disadvantage. If the building is in a geographic area that you are also not familiar with, this presents you with an even bigger disadvantage.

If you need to quickly exit a building, determine where the exits are as soon as you arrive. Make this a habit and it will become second nature to you. *You are not being paranoid; you are being safe.* It doesn't matter if there is a threat from a fire or from an active shooter—both will require you to leave quickly. Do you really care what causes you to have to leave? Of course not! That is why it pays to be aware and prepared. If something happens, you have a slight advantage and an increased chance at getting out safely. Another good habit to get into is once inside, position yourself so that you have a view of the door or one of the exits. This way if something were to occur, you will be able to see it right away and also zero in on an exit in order to leave as quickly as possible.

If you are traveling and in an unfamiliar geographic area, you will be at an additional disadvantage because you may not know what direction to go in. This could present a problem if you end up taking a wrong turn down a dead end. Any time you are planning on going to an area that you are unfamiliar with, take a few short minutes to look at it on a map. Using *Google Maps* makes this extremely easy, but do it ahead of time! If you are trying to look up something but your phone's battery is dead or you have no service, it will do you no good. Know the routes in and out of where you are going to be. When going on vacation, familiarize yourself with certain things before you go such as main roads and major landmarks. These can be of critical value should you need to evacuate an area for any number of reasons—manmade or from an act of nature.

Third, get in the habit of noticing the <u>objects</u> and things around you for potential value in the event of a problem. Certain large obstacles may be suitable for concealment, but not for cover in the event of a shooting. Also be aware of objects that can be turned into improvised weapons that can be used against an attacker. You will be amazed at how you can get creative when thinking about items as weapons and not looking at them solely for their intended function. For example, any item that has a handle can be used as a distance weapon. This can include things such as brooms, mops, rakes, and shovels. Sports equipment such as bats, lacrosse sticks and field hockey sticks can also be used. Smaller objects can be thrown at an attacker such as books, staplers, keyboards, folding chairs, etc. The goal isn't to inflict a lot of damage—the goal is to safely escape.

Other items can be sprayed or squirted into the eyes of an attacker and are readily available in a woman's purse. These include perfume, hair spray, lotions, body spray, room spray, breath spray, hand sanitizer, bug spray and other items. Hopefully there is pepper spray in there as well! If not, get some today! When deploying pepper spray or any other spray at your attacker, spray in a back and forth motion at their eyes. If they are wearing glasses, aim for their forehead so that the spray drips into their eyes. Fire extinguishers are something that exists all over college campuses and can be used as defensive weapons—first by spraying in an attacker's eyes, and then by striking them with the canister.

There are a wide variety of items that can be used to aid in defending yourself. However, weapons of any type can be taken away and used against you, so be aware of that if you decide to carry any sort of weapon. A free report that analyzes over 20 items is available on our web site titled "Self-Defense Items For Everyday Carry" by clicking this link (http://learnselfdefenseonline.com/lsdo-lc/) or by visiting http://learnselfdefenseonline.com/lsdo-lc/.

The mental side of self-defense is often overlooked. You can learn effective self-defense techniques from a book, video or qualified instructor. However, you may have a difficult time executing it if you don't have the mental fortitude to follow through with it. This requires advance preparation and asking yourself the tough questions before you need the answer. You must tell yourself "When that happens, I will do this!" and use specifics. Get in the proper "warrior mindset" that gives you the mental strength and will to overcome any obstacle or threat to your personal safety. You can watch my intro training on the Warrior Mindset on YouTube here (http://www.youtube.com/watch?v=2SnPp5jDR24) and watch the entire training by signing up for a free membership at www.LearnSelfDefenseOnline.com.

There are 5 Steps To Survive An Attack:

1. Commit—make up your mind and GO!
2. Distract—noise & commotion; kick, scream, yell!
3. Escape / Defend—use your chosen technique and execute it!
4. Attack, Attack, Attack! Do NOT let up until the threat is neutralized! Fight for your life, not your property!
5. Run—away from the situation as fast as possible & call for help!

The next section contains specific blocks, strikes and self-defense techniques that utilize the body's natural motions so they can be executed effectively with a minimal amount of training.

Blocks:

Using your arms and hands, there are 3 main blocks you should familiarize yourself with. The first is a middle block which blocks strikes and punches against the middle portion of your body. The second is the high block which effectively blocks strikes that come from above both with and without weapons. The third block is the low block which is effective against low strikes and kicks.

Middle Block:

Begin with your arm bent at your side and fist close to your ear.

Swing your arm across your centerline (center of your body) and block your opponent's punch. Twist in such a way that your block is also a strike to their wrist's radial nerve cluster located just above the wrist on the inner side. A hit to this area will cause weakness and temporary paralysis of their hand, making it an ideal target to strike during both blocks and when breaking a grab.

High Block:

The high block is a natural body movement since it only involves raising your arm up above your head. *Make sure that your arm rises straight up your centerline and doesn't swing up from the outside.*

Move inside quickly to intercept and jam the attacker's arm to prevent getting hit. The angle formed by your arm in this manner should deflect the attack down and to the outside to keep your arm from becoming broken, especially if deflecting a weapon.

Low Block:

In order to block a lower strike, kick or swinging attack, a low block is needed. Begin by bringing your fist up next to your ear on the opposite side *(left fist to right ear or vice-versa).*

Next, swing your arm down across your centerline, deflecting the attack off to the side.

Strikes:

There are dozens of ways to strike someone effectively using all different parts of the body. However, it is not necessary to learn them all. Be aware of what the main ones are and learn how to execute them correctly.

The traditional **punch** is what first comes to mind, and it is effective when done properly. The problem is that if you are a woman who has long nails, it is not possible to make a proper fist. An improperly formed punch can potentially hurt or damage your hand or wrist. The proper way to form a punch is to curl all your fingers into your palm as tightly as possible and then bring your thumb across your first 2 fingers. Ensure that your wrist is straight and aligned with your forearm. If it is not, you risk having your wrist bend forward or backward when punching which could sprain or break it. Lastly, strike the target with the first two knuckles by turning and driving *through* the target to generate maximum power and damage.

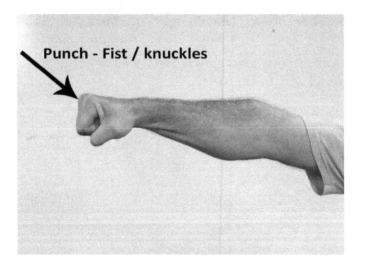

Punch - Fist / knuckles

Another closed hand strike is the **hammer fist**. As the name implies, you simply squeeze your hand together like forming a punch, but you hammer down onto the target with the bottom of your hand—the head of the hammer. You can effectively strike both hard and soft targets with it.

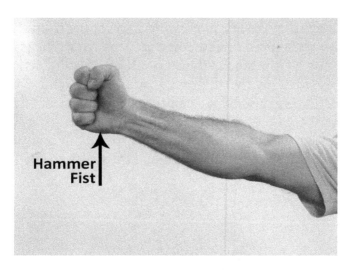

Open hand strikes are preferred in many cases for several reasons. The **tips of the fingers** and your **nails** can be used to poke and press into soft targets. Many books on self-defense teach poking the eyes, and it is effective, but could you bring yourself to poke someone's eyes out, even if you were in fear for your life? Some people may be too squeamish or unwilling to do this. Other soft targets include throat, temples and groin.

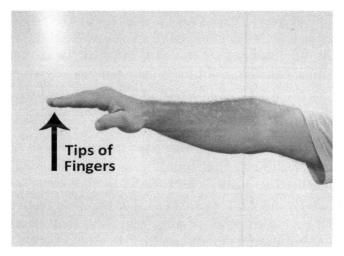

A **knife hand** strike involves using a chopping motion (karate chop) with your hand directed at a target such as the jaw below the ear, side of the neck, floating rib and groin. It is simply an open hand with the fingers close together and the thumb tucked in. The strike surface can be either the *outer* edge of the hand or in the case of a **ridge hand** strike, the striking surface is the *inner* edge of the hand. Be sure to tuck your thumb all the way into your palm during a ridge hand strike to soft targets.

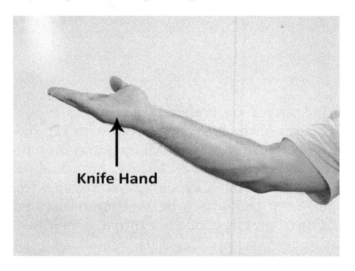

Knife Hand

Clapping an attacker's ears with **cupped hands** can damage or rupture ear drums and is a very effective defense. It will cause your attacker to experience problems with their balance when their equilibrium is affected from your attack on their ear drums. This will give you a chance to escape.

The throat is an excellent soft target that can be hit using the fingers or the **webbing of the hand** between the thumb and forefinger when the hand opens and forms the letter "L". A strike to an attacker's throat, regardless of size will be effective. Strike their throat just above the Adam's apple and then press in and drive down. No matter how big and strong an attacker is, their throat is one of the most vulnerable points on their body.

Another excellent strike using an open hand that can also be used to block kicks is a **palm strike**. As the name implies, the open hand is drawn back by bending your wrist back toward you and the palm of the hand is the point that is used to strike the attacker under the chin, driving their head back. This will force them to loosen their grip on you, allowing you to counter strike continually until they stop their attack and you can escape.

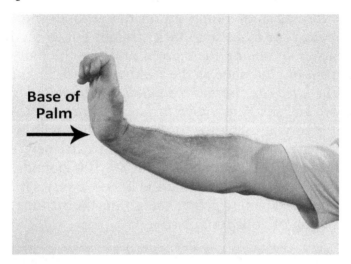

Your **elbow** is *the* hardest point on your body. Up close it is a devastatingly effective weapon that you can use to strike just about anywhere with good results. Strikes to the nose, chin, head, solar plexus, ribs and groin are all great targets to strike with the elbow. It can be used to strike both in front as well as behind you.

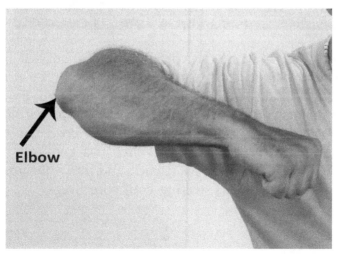

Kicks: (Your Legs Are Longer and Stronger than Your Arms—So Use Them!)

Kicks should be executed <u>low</u> so that you are less likely to lose your balance. Kicking too high increases the chance of losing your footing and ending up on the ground—not a good thing. Direct your **front snap kick** straight out to the front of your attacker's knee or their groin and use the ball of your foot or front of your shoe as the striking surface. *A kick to the front of the knee can rupture the patellar tendon and cause the knee to buckle, sending your attacker crashing to the ground.* This will give you a chance to escape as they will be unable to stand, walk or run after you. It is an extremely effective defense because it only requires about 80–100 pounds of pressure per square inch to dislocate the knee—a very serious and painful injury. When targeting the groin, the striking surface used is the <u>top</u> of your foot or shoe.

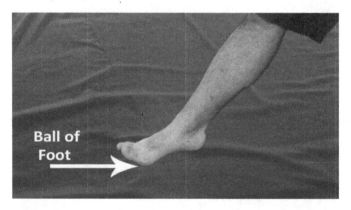

The **foot stomp** is an effective defense that can be used either in front of you or behind you. The target is the top of the attacker's foot. If using it against an attacker who is behind you, try to rake down the shin as you come down to increase the pain inflicted. If you are wearing heels, use them to focus your power on the target. A **back kick** is also very effective when attacked from behind. Lift your leg up, and then drive it back and into your attacker's knee, groin or solar plexus striking with your heel.

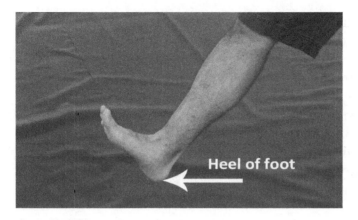

Heel of foot

Ladies, your **high heels** can inflict a significant amount of damage if you were to stomp on an attackers foot or kick them in the groin with a long, sharp heel. *You can even take off the shoes and use them as weapons.* Taking off your high heels and wielding them like a couple of daggers against an attacker might make them think twice. You will probably lose your appeal as an easy target, plus you'll also be able to run away faster!

Just like the elbow is an excellent close quarters weapon, so too is your **knee**. It is also a very hard part of your body, and can be used to effectively strike an attacker in the groin, ribs, solar plexus and face. For example, if you kick the attacker in the groin, causing them to bend down, immediately drive your knee into their face or throat. *Remember this point*: one of the automatic reactions of the body is that when kicked in the groin, the body bends forward, *but the head comes up, exposing the throat* which can be hit or kicked with devastating results.

Trips:

Once an attacker is off-balance or surprised from your initial attack or defensive move, it is much easier to knock them to the ground with a trip. The simplest and most basic trip simply involves swinging the back of your leg near your calf into the back of your attacker's knee. This will cause their leg to collapse. If you are also able to pull them down to that side by pulling on the same-side arm, or by striking them on the opposite side of their body or head at the same time, it will be easier to get them to fall down. This will allow you to escape the attack.

Throws:

When dealing with an attacker that is much larger and heavier, throwing them will not appear to be a good defense since their weight will make it difficult to throw them. *However, the secret to throwing an attacker is in using the strength of your legs and not your arms or upper body.* Grab one of their arms, step close to them and bend your knees. Then quickly straighten them, and "pop" the attacker up and over or around your hips, causing them to be thrown to the ground. Depending upon the nature of the attack, you may choose to drop them on their back or their head.

Pressure Points:

There is only so much that you can learn from a text on pressure points since someone with direct knowledge is really the only way to learn about them. In light of that statement, some general information about pressure points can definitely help you to survive.

Pressure points are areas of the body where various nerves, muscles and other vessels intersect making for greater-than-average sensitivity.

Depending upon the location, the individual, and the technique used, not only can you use them to execute a particular technique more effectively, they can be used to completely disable your attacker. *The most important thing to remember is that striking a pressure point weakens any associated muscles that area of nerves controls.* This can enable you to escape a strong grip, for example. See Appendix C: Pressure Point and Strike Charts.

Joint Manipulation:

The human body is designed to move in certain ways, and not designed to move in others. The concept of joint manipulation is such that you use this knowledge of the human body to control your attacker since everyone's body works the same way. This knowledge allows anyone, regardless of size, skill or strength, to manipulate their attacker's joints to make them move in the direction you wish. *This is a powerful concept that allows smaller people such as children, women and the elderly to overcome larger, stronger attackers.*

Part of the reason why many self-defense techniques are effective is that they take advantage of the body's various joints and manipulate them to achieve control over an attacker. Wrists are one of the easiest joints to use in order to put your adversary in a compromised position. There is an extremely satisfying feeling that comes from executing a move on your attacker that has them screaming in pain because they grabbed you and you knew how to use that to your advantage. In some cases, the stronger their grip on you, the better the technique works!

Addressing the topic of direct joint manipulation in a book is also difficult, because you are unable to really appreciate the subtle moves, angles and pressures that are necessary for you to understand in order to execute a joint manipulation technique most effectively. The same would be true if you wanted to become a chiropractor—you can't just read a book about it; you need hands-on experience and lots of practice.

The great advantage of performing a joint lock is that allows you to:

a) cause them pain so they stop their attack or
b) hold them as you execute a strike or
c) continue the technique until the joint is broken or
d) dislocate the joint.

That is the power that comes with proper execution of joint locks, manipulations and throws involving joints.

Students of self-defense who are interested in learning more are encouraged to contact a local martial arts school that teaches these techniques such as Korean *Hapkido* or Japanese *Aikido* and *Jiu Jitsu*. These are considered "soft" martial arts because they teach you how to redirect your opponent's energy and defend yourself in such a way that you gain the advantage. These sorts of self-defense techniques should be taught in person by someone with many years of experience. <u>Don't try to learn them on your own with a friend. One of you may end up seriously injured because you were not taught the proper and safe way to execute a move when practicing.</u>

Part 2: Safe Dating & Rape Prevention

Dating in college is part of growing up and developing into a young adult. The more people you meet and date, the greater the chances that you may experience some form of dating violence. Safe dating needs to be practiced when meeting someone for the first time. Bring along a friend or two and meet in a safe, public place with lots of people present.

Keep in mind that dating violence can involve more than just the physical act of violence toward another person. The obvious types of physical abuse such as slapping, shoving, biting, grabbing, etc. are not the only problems. Using weapons such as knives and guns to threaten someone and potentially force them into being sexually assaulted or raped can also be an issue. Non-physical threats including stalking and cyber-stalking are also unnerving for the victim. *Any harassment where the intent is to coerce or abuse another may also be construed as dating violence.*

The problem is not isolated; several studies conducted on college campuses around the country report that 1 in 5 students who have been in a serious relationship report being hit, slapped or pushed. *This means that around 20 percent of all relationships during college involved some sort of physical abuse.* These are shocking statistics that should serve as a wake-up call to all college students and their parents. The US Department of Justice has also reported on extremely high incidents of dating violence. (http://www.cdc.gov/violenceprevention/pdf/schoolviolence_factsheet-a.pdf)

Dating violence, or intimate partner violence (IPV) is any sort of controlling or abusive behavior that exists in a dating situation or romantic relationship. It can happen in both heterosexual as well as LGBT relationships. The violence or abuse can take various forms including one or more forms of verbal, emotional, physical or sexual abuse. This same Department of Justice survey found that one in three women, one in ten men, and one in two transgender individuals are victims of dating violence.

Many times the term "date rape" is used, but in all reality (and according to many experts) the more appropriate term is "drug-facilitated sexual assault." This is because in many instances of sexual assault, drugs are used to help the perpetrators carry out the crime.

When only women are studied, more than 10% report being stalked during their time in college, and about 25% of that stalking is conducted through various online social media sites and electronic devices. The numbers are truly staggering when realize that between 20% to 30% of women will experience some type of sexual assault during their 4-year college career.

These are only reported numbers; many incidents are never reported, either by the victims or by the institutions where they occur. We can conclude that the rates are higher than what are typically reported.

Every year in the United States 3.4 million people are stalked. The majority are between the ages of 18–24, and 3 out of 4 are stalked by someone they know, not a stranger. If you are being stalked, contact the police and get a protection from abuse (PFA) order if necessary. Save any evidence you have to build a strong case with dates and times. If you are a victim of dating violence, visit the following link for help: https://www .womenshealth.gov/violence-against-women/types-of-violence/ stalking.html

The following are summarized scenarios outlined by S.A.V.E. (Students Against Violence Everywhere; http://nationalsave .org/) regarding dating violence.

1. You may be dating someone who is jealous and possessive, does not allow you to have friends, and is constantly keeping tabs on you. They will not accept it if you try to end the relationship. They could attempt to isolate you from your family and friends in order to make you dependent on them and keep you from leaving.

2. They make every attempt to control you by telling you what to do, where to go, what to wear, etc. They also don't allow you to make decisions for yourself as well as not take what you have to say seriously. Their verbal and emotional abuse toward you can end up damaging your self-esteem and make you doubt your abilities as a person and a partner. They may want to get serious quickly.

3. They may embarrass, threaten or scare you to the point where you think twice before speaking your mind or saying something because of fear of reprisal or physical harm. If this person has access to guns or other weapons, or has threatened you with them in the past, you will be intimidated. You will be more afraid to stand up for yourself because of the threat of injury or death.

4. Your partner may have damaged property, abused animals or other partners in the past, have a history of fighting or be quick to lose their temper. They may brag about things they have done in the past such as forcing someone to do something against their will.

5. They may blame you for everything and fail to take any responsibility for their actions. When confronted, they will deny, deflect or rationalize the things they have done to make them seem like they were fine or no big deal.
6. They may have a misconstrued or out-of-touch interpretation about how relationships are supposed to be. This could include them feeling that one of the people in the relationship needs to be in charge, and the other needs to be subservient. They may force you to perform sexual acts against your will. This may stem from things that they experienced during their childhood or upbringing.

Key factors to look for in your partner are:

• Extreme Jealousy
• Possessiveness
• Emotional Abuse
• Physical Abuse
• Explosive Anger
• Mood Swings
• Alcohol and Drug Use/Abuse

There is a cycle or circle of violence that occurs among these people:

A) Tension builds up
B) Violence erupts in a variety of forms
C) Seduce the victim to stay with them and then back to A)

Basically, the way it works is that when you are first in the relationship, everything is going fine. You like the person you are with, they seem to be a great guy or girl, and for a while things are normal. However, as time goes on, little things begin to bother one of those in the relationship and the tension begins to build. As these tensions build, one of the above six scenarios may begin to play out.

Eventually, there will be a violent outburst—verbal, emotional, and/or physical—and damage or injury may be done to the victim at this time.

After this outburst, the person will apologize and attempt to make amends, saying it won't happen again, they don't know why they did what they did, etc. This is an attempt to lull their partner into a false sense of security and believe they can get that person to stay in the relationship out of love, hope or fear. Many victims will stay in the relationship, even if it is abusive because they do love the other person and believe they will change. They hope that the other person's promises are genuine and that they will adhere to them. The other reason is that they are simply afraid to leave because they don't know what the other person may be capable of doing to them if they try to break off the relationship.

If you find yourself in a relationship as described here, be *very* careful and recognize what is happening around you and to you. Do not get caught up in the cycle of violence that being in a relationship of this sort produces. You may find it necessary to speak with someone at your school about the problem. In extreme cases, tell the police if you feel that you are in danger of physical harm or in fear for your life. Do not wait! Many victims thought that the other person would change or that things would be different "this time." Don't be fooled—get help and get out! For more in-depth information, statistics and more including a dating violence quiz, visit http://www.NationalSave.org

As we discussed in previous chapters, there is a very real digital threat to dating violence. This form of "digital dating abuse" includes things similar to cyber-bullying like sending unwanted messages or images to the victim. The abuser may also pressure the victim to send explicit photos and/or videos to them. It also includes repeated behavior that can be obsessive such as sending dozens of texts per hour wanting to know every move that the victim makes.

Refrain from posting location updates in your social media accounts; this will make it easier for the other person to know exactly where you are and find you. You should also ask your friends before checking them in with you at any location simply because they may also be wary of letting someone know exactly where there are at a particular time. It can be dangerous, so I would highly recommend against using this feature on any social media. Since you are basically telling everyone where you are, it makes it very easy to not only find you, but to potentially rob you since you are not home—and telling them about it! *For your safety and security, refrain from using the check-in feature.*

The use of social media with regard to this sort of dating abuse cannot be overstated. Abusers may demand that their victims unfriend certain people on *Facebook* or stop following people on *Twitter* that the abuser perceives as a threat to the relationship. They may use social media to abuse you by sending you insulting or threatening messages.

Abusers may even want you to give them your passwords to various accounts that you have—social media, financial, etc. It should be obvious, but never under any circumstances give your login information or passwords to anyone! They will want to look through your accounts, phone records, text history, etc. in an attempt to find something suspicious because they are so obsessed and abusive. If your partner cannot trust you and respect your privacy, this is a pretty solid sign that you are in a bad relationship. You should end it as soon as you can and as amicably as possible. *The longer you stay in, the harder it will be to get out.*

If you find yourself being attacked and end up on the ground where you may be sexually assaulted or raped, it is imperative that you escape by any means necessary. The following self-defense technique will help you.

Should an attacker knock you on the ground and get on top of you, they may be choking you or striking you. You must first clear your airway.

First, distract your attacker. Scream, spit, scratch, etc.

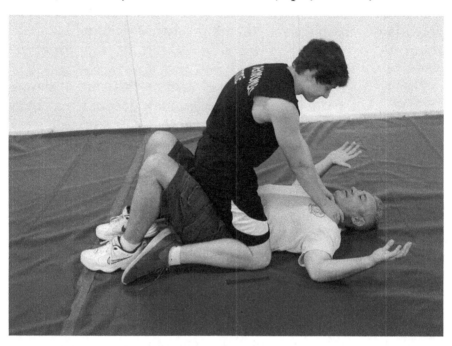

Next, chop your attacker's arms and grab one of their arms

Thrust your hips up and in the direction you wish to go.

Continue to roll to that side and . . .

. . . up onto your knees.

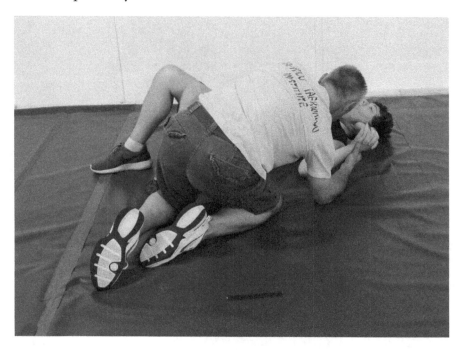

(Opposite angle shown for clarity) Then raise your hand up . . .

. . . and strike their groin.

Escape quickly!

Part 3: Alternative Lifestyle Risks

There has been a surge in activity in the LGBT community as those with alternative lifestyles and sexual preferences become more commonplace. Typically, LGBT students at college experience greater instances of sexual violence and bullying. Lesbian, gay, bisexual and transgender students experience this at a much higher rate than their heterosexual peers.

According to a Centers for Disease Control and Prevention report (https://www.cdc.gov/nchs/nhis/index.htm), LGBT students were more than three times as likely to be forced to have sex and more than twice as likely to experience violence during dates. These findings were from a *2015 National Youth Risk Behavior Survey* that looked at 118 health behaviors. It found that 23% of LGBT students reported dating violence and 18% were physically forced to have sex. It also found that 34% of the students were bullied at school and 28% were bullied online. By comparison, only 19% of heterosexual students were bullied at school and 14% online.

LGBT students were also at greater risk of destructive behavior with more than 40% having considered suicide and 12% had actually attempted suicide in the past year. They were also more than five times as likely to use illegal drugs.

So what can be done? The importance of support by schools, the community and family of these people is essential. There also must be public health and school policies that supports safe places for these students and educational programs for their families and friends.

Chapter 12 Checklist: Physical Threat
Self-Defense / Safe Dating / Sexual Harassment
/ Rape Prevention / Tolerance

✓ Threats of physical harm or sexual assault demand a decisive and immediate response. You must make sure that you know this and are mentally and physically prepared before the need arises.

✓ There are some simple self-defense principles that anyone can learn to effectively defend themselves against a larger, stronger attacker if they simply understand a few basic principles and learn how to apply them.

✓ Being aware of the <u>people</u> around you at all times is imperative. If someone looks out of place either by the way they are acting or by what they are wearing, that should signal to you that you should probably keep an eye on them or even vacate the area and alert someone to your suspicions.

✓ The <u>environment</u> you are in plays a large role in your personal safety. If you are in an unfamiliar building or a club that you are at for the first time, you are already at an immediate disadvantage.

✓ If you need to quickly exit a building, determine where the exits are as soon as you get there. It doesn't matter if there is a threat from a fire or from an active shooter—both will require you to leave quickly.

✓ If you are traveling in an unfamiliar geographic area, you will be at a disadvantage because you may not know what direction to go in.

✓ Know the routes in and out of where you are going to be.

✓ If you are going on vacation, familiarize yourself with certain things before you go such as main roads and major landmarks. These can be of critical value should you need to evacuate an area for any number of reasons—man-made or from an act of nature.

✓ Get in the habit of noticing the <u>objects</u> and things around you for potential value in the event of a problem.

✓ Items that can be sprayed or squirted into the eyes of an attacker are readily available in a woman's purse such as perfume, hair spray, lotions, hand sanitizer and others.

✓ You can learn effective self-defense techniques, yet you may have a difficult time executing it if you don't have the mental fortitude to follow through with it.

✓ Get in the proper "warrior mindset" that gives you the mental strength and will to overcome any obstacle or threat to your personal safety.

✓There are 5 Steps To Survive An Attack:

1. Commit—make up your mind and GO!
2. Distract—noise & commotion; kick, scream, yell!
3. Escape / Defend—use your chosen technique and execute it!
4. Attack, Attack, Attack! Do NOT let up until the threat is neutralized!
5. Run—away from the situation as fast as possible & call for help

✓ Your elbow is the hardest point on your body.
✓ Your legs are longer and stronger than your arms—so use them!
✓ Kicks should be executed low so that you don't lose your balance.
✓ A kick to the front of the knee can rupture the patellar tendon and cause the knee to buckle, sending your attacker crashing to the ground.
✓ When targeting the groin, the striking surface used is the top of your foot.
✓ Ladies, your high heels can inflict a significant amount of damage if you stomp an attackers foot or kick them in the groin with a long, sharp heel.
✓ The knee is also a very hard part of your body, and can be used to effectively strike an attacker in the groin, ribs, solar plexus and face.
✓ Pressure points are areas of the body where various nerves, muscles and other vessels intersect making for greater-than-average sensitivity.
✓ Striking a pressure point weakens any associated muscles that area of nerves controls.
✓ LGBT students are more than 3 times as likely to be forced to have sex and more than twice as likely to experience violence during dates.

CHAPTER 13

Active Shooter Preparedness & Defensive Actions

Random shootings used to be just that—random. A generation ago they were few and far between. Two generations ago they were almost non-existent. For this generation, that is unfortunately no longer the case.

With increasing frequency we are forced to read and watch the news as school shootings, acts of terrorism, and bombs disrupt our lives and change the lives of the victims and their families forever. The sheer number of these occurrences has begun to desensitize us as a society simply due to the frequency with which they are happening. Since 2006, the US has averaged an active shooter event, which is defined as one with four or more deaths, approximately every three months.

So just what is the definition of an "active shooter?" Although definitions may vary slightly, *it is an individual who is actively attempting to shoot and kill people in a populated, and sometimes confined area.*

Places that fit the definition of populated and confined and that are targeted by active shooters include:

- Workplace—51% occur at work
- Schools—17% occur in schools
- Public Places—17% occur in stores, malls, movie theaters, etc.
- Religious Places—6% occur in churches, synagogues, & temples

When we see things on the news that do not directly affect us, we typically don't pay it much attention other than the initial reports. We have lives of our own and problems that demand our immediate attention. If something doesn't directly affect us, we go on with our busy lives. Victims are usually chosen by random and happen to be in the wrong place at the wrong time.

We know that incidents of gun violence will undoubtedly occur in the future. The yearly average for mass shootings is now a whopping 20 per year! Knowing what to do when it erupts near us or to us needs to be a priority for every responsible person. Simply avoiding the issue or denying that it can happen is not a solution. In fact, it is worse to deny that a potential problem may exist because that will put you at greater risk. Therefore, we must prepare by learning about and practicing specific strategies that should be put into effect at the appropriate time. Proactive preparation may actually prevent a problem from happening to you and is much preferred over a reactive response. Avoidance is the best solution!

Of course, we can't always avoid a problem and so the following are the 3 steps to take during an active shooter event.

1. Avoid / Run—if possible, get out as fast as you can. Think about, plan and visualize where you are running to before you move. Have a destination to focus on. *Stay low as you rapidly move to the closest exit in a zig-zag pattern to be a tougher target to hit.* Keep your hands up as much as possible so that law enforcement doesn't mistake you for the shooter as you exit. Have an exit plan.

   Anything can be used as an exit in an emergency, so don't just limit your thinking to doors. Windows are a viable option if you are on the ground level and they can be opened or easily broken by throwing a chair or other object through them. If you are in a public place such as a mall or restaurant, keep in mind that most stores have a back entrance or exit for deliveries. You can take stairs up or down to get away from the threat. If you can help others, do so but not at the risk of your own personal safety. You must move away from the source of the threat as quickly as you are able. Get distance and cover between you and the shooter.

   Also be cognizant of the risk and be able to articulate to first responders as much information as you can provide.

Do not put yourself at risk, but notice as much as you can as you get out. Let law enforcement or campus security know where the risk is, how many people are involved and any other relevant information such as what room they were in, what direction they were heading, what they look like, what they are wearing, how many shooters there are, etc. <u>Be a good witness.</u>

2. Deny / Hide—if the exit is blocked and you are unable to escape, your next best course of action will be to lockdown and hide—quietly! *Silence your cell phone or anything else that can make noise.* Consider in advance where you should hide. Turn off all lights. If at all possible get away from doors and windows and hide behind cover.

   Do *whatever you can in an attempt to deny the shooter access to your location.* Lock and barricade the door using anything you can. Move desks and chairs in the way of any entry points, but try to do so with a <u>minimal amount of noise.</u> Know the difference between cover and concealment. Cover can stop a bullet—concealment will only hide you. It is imperative that you know the difference because only <u>cover</u> will provide you with protection from bullets. In the absence of cover, concealment will have to do. Stay quiet and out of sight and hope that the shooter doesn't see you or come upon your location. If they do, then you have no choice but to fight.

   Keep in mind that the majority of active shooter situations are over within 15 minutes. This may not sound like a long time, but if you are hiding and waiting to see if you are passed over by a maniac intent on killing you and others, it can seem like an eternity. <u>Do not leave the safety of your lock-down location until and unless you are certain that the threat is no longer in the area or has been neutralized.</u>

3. Defend / Fight—when you can't escape and run away, and your hiding place is compromised, there will be no alternative but to fight. This is your last resort . . . if you have other options, use them. You must understand that this decision will be one that could very well be the most difficult thing you have ever done and possibly

the last decision of your life. *However, you simply cannot just wait helplessly to be killed in cold blood.*

You must turn into a warrior (see Warrior Mindset [https://www.youtube.com/watch?v=2SnPp5jDR24] and Chapter 16 Part 3) that will accept nothing less than victory in this decision. <u>There can be no hesitation.</u> Every primal emotion and all of your adrenaline must be focused on one thing and that is your very survival. If you have others with you, everyone must attack viciously at once and overwhelm the shooter.

Think about all that you have to live for. No one has the right to take your life! Choose to live or die on your own terms! If you are going to die, at least decide to go out fighting. Remember that *if you are aware enough to know that you are wounded, you are aware enough to keep fighting.* You have to get primal—there are no rules and no such thing as fighting "fair" when you are fighting for your life! Gouging eyes, punching/clawing the throat, kicking the groin or knees, etc. are all valid when your life is on the line.

Use anything around you than can be turned into a weapon to gain some advantage. Anything that can be used to impair the shooter's ability to see, breathe or control their weapon is what you are looking for. Things like fire extinguishers can be used to blind the attacker and then you can hit them with it. A variety of items in a woman's purse can be used to temporary blind the shooter including perfume, hair spray and bug spray. Brooms, mops, umbrellas, canes, rakes and shovels can all be used as effective weapons against an attacker. Primary targets are the back of the head, eyes, nose, throat, solar plexus, groin and knees. A good rule is to follow the center-line of the body.

Any hard objects such as books, cell phones, keyboards, laptops, monitors, chairs, floor fans, garbage cans—*anything and everything you can find must be looked at as a potential weapon that could be used to defend yourself.* Laptops & the power supply "bricks" on the end of their power cords make excellent weapons to swing at an attacker. Who cares if you break your laptop or power supply over their head?

At least you will be alive and can buy another laptop, but there is no buying another you!

When help arrives (and it will!) try to do your best to remain calm and follow their instructions. Drop anything you are holding and raise your empty hands high in the air to show arriving officers there is nothing in them! *This is very important since police and SWAT officers are trained to look at your hands for potential weapons/threats.* Move slowly and do not make any sudden movements that could startle the officers. Do not touch or attempt to hug the officers/responders. Continue past them in the direction they came from and exit in an orderly manner until you are clear of the threat.

Be prepared to provide information to the responders such as the location of the shooter(s), how many there are, the weapons they have, their clothing description, and the number of potential victims.

Being aware of how others around you are acting can sometimes alert you to the fact that *something just isn't "right."* In many cases involving active shooters, there are some commonalities that have been documented.

The following are some of the more common traits exhibited by people who ended up becoming active shooters or perpetrators of violence.

- They change from "normal" to strange, radical, withdrawn, verbally abusive or intolerant almost overnight.
- They could be described as a "loner" with no apparent social life, friends or relationships.
- They may have recently experienced a job loss or lost a loved one.
- They have no interests, hobbies or leisure activities.
- They have recently acquired an acute interest in conspiracies or radical ideas to the point where they are consumed by them.
- Their general appearance is typically sloppy; they do not put a lot of effort into their personal hygiene, dress or overall look.

- They typically have problems with authority and are unable to accept criticism without lashing out, getting angry or worse.
- Their mood can swing wildly from benevolent to hostile or withdrawn rapidly and for no apparent reason.
- They make violent and disturbing threats against others with no thought about the recourse of their potential actions.
- They may be "set off" by something seemingly minor which causes them to have physically violent outbursts where they scream, curse, throw things, break things, etc.
- They may have completely irrational disagreements with others at work or in social settings.
- They may demonstrate severe bias toward those who differ in opinion, religion, social status, race or other group.

This is by no means a complete list, but it serves to demonstrate that a person may begin to exhibit certain behaviors that they did not previously.

To an observant person, such as a co-worker or classmate, this should warrant additional concern and a heightened sense of awareness with regard to this individual. You can speak to a manager or boss at work and voice your concerns. At school, find a teacher, guidance counselor or your campus security department and let them know your thoughts about anyone who is exhibiting strange behavior that could be cause for alarm.

It is better to be proactive and stop a potential problem by being overly concerned than to ignore a potential problem before it is too late.

Some other things to watch for include those engaging in suspicious behavior such as looking nervously from side to side, constantly patting a location on their person to ensure "something" is there, wearing clothing that is out of season such as a trench coat when it's 90 degrees out, etc.

Observe people and notice the little things. Is someone walking in a dazed manner or do they appear expressionless and oblivious to what is going on around them? Do they avert their eyes when you try to make eye contact?

If you notice something or someone that appears odd or out of place, let your college public safety department know or call local law enforcement. It is better to be overly cautious and have it turn out to be nothing than to ignore a potential problem and end up having it turn out to be something.

Don't be the person that looks back and reflects after an event and realizes that there was something that you noticed by failed to mention to the authorities. Report suspicious behavior and be observant, vigilant and careful. You may just end up saving yourself as well as many other innocent people from a deadly attack!

The goal is to be constantly in a heightened state of awareness, not paranoia. Viewing everyone as a potential threat isn't the goal, but noticing the ones who are acting strange or appear out of place is.

The reality is that the chances of you being involved in a random shooting are pretty remote—about one in a million. Does that mean you should not do any advance preparation? Of course not. It is no different than preparing for any other type of disaster such as a fire, flood, hurricane, tornado, earthquake, hazardous material spill, nuclear disaster, terror attack, etc.

Keep in mind the main points in the above outline and hope for the best—but be prepared for the worst.

Chapter 13 Checklist: Active Shooter Defensive Actions

✓ The 3 steps to take during an active shooter event:

1. Avoid / Run—if possible, get out as fast as you can. Think about, plan and visualize where you are running to before you move. Have a destination to focus on. Anything can be used as an exit in an emergency, so don't just limit your thinking to doors. Windows are a viable option if you are on the ground level and they can be opened or easily broken by throwing a chair or other object through them.
2. Deny / Hide—if the exit is blocked and you are unable to escape, your next best course of action will be to lock-down and hide—quietly! Silence your cell phone or anything else

that can make noise. Turn off all lights. Get away from doors and windows and hide behind cover. Do whatever you can in an attempt to deny the shooter access to your location. Lock and barricade the door using anything you can to keep the shooter out.

3. Defend / Fight—when you can't escape and run away, and your hiding place is compromised, there will be no alternative but to fight. There can be no hesitation. Every primal emotion and all of your adrenaline must be focused on one thing and that is your very survival. If you have others with you, everyone must attack viciously at once and overwhelm the shooter. Be committed!

✓ Observe people and notice the little things. It is better to be proactive and stop a potential problem by being overly concerned than to ignore a potential problem before it is too late.

✓ Don't be the person that looks back and reflects after an event and realizes that there was something that you noticed but failed to mention to the authorities. Report suspicious behavior and be observant, vigilant and careful.

✓ Hope for the best—but be prepared for the worst.

CHAPTER 14

Terrorism

The subject of terrorism is one we are confronted with more frequently. Those living in countries where the specter of terrorism was never an issue such as the United States are getting a taste of what other countries have been dealing with for years.

Terrorism is a very real problem for colleges in the United States as well as those abroad for several reasons. As we witnessed in November 2016, the attack at Ohio State University was perpetrated by a radically inspired Islamist extremist. He used his car and a knife to injure 12 innocent people that included students, faculty and staff of the school.

College campuses have increasingly become targets for terrorist attacks in recent years. Data from the searchable *University of Maryland Global Terrorism Database* (http://www.start.umd.edu/gtd/) shows a sharp increase in terrorist attacks on educational institutions around the world since 2005. In fact, more than 3400 terrorist attacks in 110 countries targeted educational institutions from 1970–2013.

The average number of global attacks from 1970 until 2005 ranged between 20–100 per year. However, since 2005, the number of attacks has sharply increased, surpassing 200 in 2009 and spiking up to 371 in 2013 (the last year data was recorded). This is an increase of over 300% in less than 5 years! *In all, a total of over 150,000 international terrorist attacks have been recorded from 1970 through 2015.* This site is an excellent resource that is updated annually with various data on terror attacks.

The FBI has also weighed in on the problem, issuing warnings that schools and universities in the United States are "soft" targets that are vulnerable to terrorist attacks.

The reasons for this include the following as summarized by Rick Amweg and Paul Denton in their article, "Why

Terrorists Target Colleges and Universities." (http://www
.campussafetymagazine.com/article/why_terrorists_target
_colleges_campus_universities/blog)

1. Schools and universities contain many targets in addition
   to the obvious high concentrations of people on campus.
   They often also contain research labs, medical facilities,
   historic architecture and collections of artwork. All are
   attractive targets.
2. Colleges are symbols of freedom, education and democracy and since terrorists' goals include suppressing education and freedom, they feel threatened by anything that
   can challenge their ideology.
3. College campuses are popular places to host workshops,
   concerts, sporting events and political events. A terrorist
   attack during a major event would bring attention to their
   cause and has the potential for lots of casualties. They
   are also not as secure as government facilities or other
   locations.
4. Universities are hosting increasing numbers of foreign students. These students come from many foreign countries,
   including ones that are known to provide funding for terrorists. As these numbers increase, so does the potential
   for terrorists posing as students to enter the country with
   student visas. The systems in place to do the vetting for
   these students can be improved, and so this is an area of
   valid concern.
5. Finally, college campuses are typically geographically large
   and spread out with limited security in most areas. The
   college library and cafeteria may be open to the public,
   so that anyone may gain access. In addition, large numbers of people move around campus in between classes so
   the potential for mass casualties is great. It also makes it
   easy for non-student terrorists to blend in, especially as the
   number of foreign students increases as mentioned above.

One of the most dangerous threats to personal safety on
college campuses from terrorist attacks come from what have
been termed the "lone wolf." These are individuals who are not

directly affiliated with any organized terror group, but believe in the ideals and causes that they stand for. They are nearly impossible to spot until it becomes evident during an attack.

These people are influenced by various factors including religious ideologies, political motivations, racial biases, environmental extremism or other specific factors. They decide to take matters into their own hands in the name of something. Their goal is to cause as much damage and death as they can before becoming a martyr or escaping.

Terrorism is something new to many of us, but the time to be vigilant and aware of the problem is now. Be careful about what you say and who you say it to at school, at work and any time you are out in public. You never know who might be listening.

Chapter 14 Checklist: Terrorism

✓ College campuses have increasingly become targets for terrorist attacks in recent years
✓ More than 3400 terrorist attacks in 110 countries targeted educational institutions from 1970–2013
✓ Since 2005, the number of attacks has sharply increased
✓ Schools and universities contain many targets in addition to the obvious high concentrations of people on campus
✓ Colleges are symbols of freedom, education and democracy which threaten the terrorists and can challenge their ideology
✓ College campuses are popular places to host workshops, concerts, sporting events and political event and are not as secure as government facilities or other locations
✓ Universities are hosting increasing numbers of foreign students who can blend in easily and post as students.
✓ College campuses are typically geographically large and spread out with limited security in most areas where large numbers of people move around making the potential for mass casualties great.

Building Self-Confidence

Lack of self-confidence can be a real problem. It is easy to doubt one's physical abilities if we are told repeatedly that we are dumb, slow, fat, thin, ugly, short, etc. We may also doubt our mental abilities in our study habits, lab work, or test taking. If someone is awkward in a social setting, the lack of confidence will only make it worse. To top it off, lack of self-confidence is sure to draw unwanted attention from bullies or others who are looking to take advantage of them. This can cause physical, financial or emotional harm from others. Victims can be forced to do something they shouldn't do, but were talked into doing. It is because they lack the confidence to say no when asked. A perfect example of this would be a person who is approached by another person and basically told to do something they shouldn't. It could be something as seemingly harmless as giving up their seat or as harmful as giving up their dreams.

If I asked you if you wanted to be a confident person, chances are you would say "yes." However, only addressing confidence on a cursory level will not cut it. You need to be specific as with any goal in life. Just like saying "I want to be rich" will not make it so, neither will saying "I want to be confident." *You must do something about it.*

Every single person requires confidence, but in different ways. For example, a college student needs to have confidence in their ability to effectively present a project before their class. A small child may need the confidence required to memorize and deliver a line for an upcoming school play. The busy executive needs confidence in order to present their revolutionary idea to the company's board of directors. An employee requires confidence in their abilities before quitting their job to start their own business. The list and number of examples goes on and on.

Confidence is required in order to address and deal with a multitude of challenges that life throws your way. They include how you deal with everyone—classmates, friends, family, boss, co-workers, and girlfriend/boyfriend.

The following "Confidence Quiz" will help you gauge your level of confidence. Answer them truthfully with a simple YES or NO. No one is watching! You will gain valuable insight into your level of confidence . . . or your lack of it.

Confidence Quiz (Yes or No)

1. Do you have difficulty making decisions without first consulting others for their input and insights?
2. Do you feel like you need a support system made up of other people around you in order to feel secure?
3. During meetings or group discussions, do you only listen and rarely contribute?
4. At your workplace, do you refrain from speaking out about problems to your boss or manager or do you keep good ideas to yourself that could improve how the business operates?
5. Does the thought of meeting someone new terrify you?
6. Does the concept of speaking before a roomful of people make you want to run and hide?
7. Do you accept additional responsibilities because you are unable to say no—even when you are already swamped?
8. Are you extremely concerned about what other people think of you or how they view you?
9. Are you afraid of taking risks?
10. Are you dissatisfied with your outward appearance and looks?
11. Do social gatherings make you uncomfortable, as well as being around large numbers of people?

If you answered "yes" to many or even all of the answers to this quiz, you would appear to have somewhat of a "confidence crisis." This could be an obstacle to your future successes—both in business and in life. There is no need to panic, however! *Being aware that a problem exists is the first step toward rectifying it.* You need to take action and work to build up your self-confidence. It will make you more successful—and safer!

If you answered "no" to most of these questions, then good for you! You seem to be a pretty confident person, but be aware! Being overly confident can be perceived as cocky, so it is a fine line between the two. Know when to ask for help, and know when you don't know something! Many times an overly confident person allows their confidence to morph into cockiness, and that is a turn-off for everyone around you. Nobody likes a know-it-all, and if you pretend to know something that you really don't, it will come back to you in a very negative way.

The next step for those who lack confidence is to begin to understand that you have plenty of things that you have accomplished in your life to this point that can help boost your confidence levels. If you are a college student (and if you're reading this you probably are!) then simply being accepted into college and attending is something to be proud of! There are plenty of people who apply and do not get accepted, so reflect on that for a few minutes.

In order to keep building your confidence, ask yourself the following questions, again with a simple yes/no answer.

1. Have you accomplished *anything* in the past? (I bet you have!)
2. When entering a new place, or when you're around new people, do you wait for someone to talk to you, or do you approach them?
3. Do you feel that others respect you?
4. Do you believe that you have the potential to be successful?
5. Are you generally a happy and loving person?
6. Are you satisfied with your chosen career path or major?
7. Are you satisfied with the skills you've already acquired as well as those you're currently learning?
8. Do you feel like you are in control of your life?
9. Do you imagine yourself as more successful in five years?
10. Do you feel like you are worthy of success?

If you answered most of this second set of questions with a "no" then you do have low self-confidence, but that can change! Nothing is set in stone, and you are in control of your own life, believe it or not. Life does not "happen" to you. You make decisions every single day that change the course of your life for better or worse. Where you are today is the result of decisions that you made in the past. Where you will be tomorrow will be the result of the decisions you make today and in the days, weeks, months and years ahead.

If you lack certain skills, go out and learn them! If you are not satisfied with your chosen career path, then change it! You must believe that you are in control of your own destiny because you most certainly are. You must believe that you are worthy of success because everyone is! We all have similar challenges that cause problems and may force us to deviate from our desired outcomes. However, having a clearly defined goal that is made up of small, measurable steps is the key to moving forward.

There will always be challenges, roadblocks and curve balls thrown your way. You must decide whether or not you are going to let them stop you or not, and that is a decision that no one can make for you. Watch the Warrior Mindset (https://www.youtube.com/watch?v=2SnPp5jDR24)   training that is mentioned in the next chapter—it will give you strength and help motivate you to work through any challenges you may face on your journey in this wild ride called "life!"

Going hand-in-hand with a lack of confidence is anxiety. Typically having anxiety about a situation, person, project or anything for that matter will cause you to be fearful, anxious and anything but confident. *The secret to managing your anxiety is to use visualization techniques.* This simply involves you visualizing or imagining yourself successfully performing anything that is causing you anxiety. It could be an upcoming test, a big sports game you are playing in, a conversation you need to have with a friend, or anything you are feeling anxious about. The key is to imagine yourself successfully taking that test, playing the game of your life, or a positive outcome to a dreaded conversation. Tapping into these visualization techniques will help quell your anxieties.

Fear is the enemy, but remember what FEAR stands for:

F—False
E—Evidence
A—Appearing
R—Real

If you fear something, many times you are giving it more credence than it deserves—false evidence. However, that does not make it appear any less real to you, and so the vicious cycle begins. Until and unless you have proof about something, being afraid of it only fuels your fears. Do not give in to unsubstantiated fear! Fear can be a good thing when the situation warrants it—but unless there is a reason to fear something, there is no need to.

A great way to help reduce your anxiety and improve your confidence is to create a list of things that you are thankful for—your gratitude list. Having this allows you to develop an "attitude of gratitude" (Watch my video at https://www.youtube.com/watch?v=ybI4u1yEQoU) that forces you to be thankful for all the things in your life that you may take for granted. It reminds you of what is important in life—things like your family, your home, your health and your friends. Things like tests and games and other things that may be causing you to be anxious should pale in comparison to them! It will help put your life and any challenges that you may be facing in perspective. It will also enable you to reduce or eliminate the attention that you have been placing on these things so that you can focus on what is truly important.

Another way to improve your self-confidence is dress nicely and keep yourself neatly groomed. Wearing faded, wrinkled clothes and not showering for 2 days are not doing your self-confidence any favors!

Your posture is another key indicator of your confidence or lack of it. Standing up straight, shoulders back and eyes forward projects a confident person. Slouching down, shoulders rounded and eyes down projects the image of someone who lacks the confidence to stand tall and look the world in the face. It will improve your mood and also your confidence.

Procrastination is something that will definitely affect your self-confidence. If you procrastinate, you will not finish tasks—small and large. Not getting things done may cause you to view yourself as not successful because you are not getting things done. Avoid temptations and distractions so that you can focus on the tasks at hand and build confidence. Start with little things like making your bed! One achievement will lead to the next and you will get in the habit of getting things done. If you fail at something, do not dwell on it! You will fail from time to time—everyone does. You need to learn from your mistakes and try again until you do succeed. When you do accomplish something or succeed at a task, it will make you feel good, and will have a direct positive effect on your confidence. Note your accomplishments and recognize your personal worth. Seeing what you get done and feeling good about yourself will improve your confidence—period!

Often a lack of confidence stems from low self-esteem which comes from the self-image. Your self-image is the way that you see yourself. If you see yourself as a successful, confident and attractive person, the world will also see you that way. If your self-image is poor, then nothing you do in an outward sense will change that; you must begin to view yourself differently.

Chapter 15 Checklist: Building Self-Confidence

✓ Lack of self-confidence is sure to draw unwanted attention from bullies or others who are looking to take advantage of you.

✓ You need to take action and work to build up your self-confidence. It will make you more successful—and safer!

✓ Being overly confident can be perceived as cocky; it is a fine line.

✓ If you lack confidence you must understand that there are plenty of things that you have accomplished in your life to this point. Reflecting on this can help boost your confidence levels.

✓ You are in control of your own life, believe it or not.

✓ Life does not "happen" to you—you make decisions every single day that change the course of your life for better or for worse.

✓ Going hand-in-hand with a lack of confidence is anxiety. The secret to managing your anxiety is to use visualization techniques.

✓ Fear is the enemy, but remember what FEAR stands for:

> F—False
> E—Evidence
> A—Appearing
> R—Real

✓ Fear can be a good thing when the situation warrants it—but unless there is a reason to fear something, there is no need to.

✓ A great way to help reduce your anxiety and improve your confidence is to create a list of things that you are thankful for—your gratitude list.

✓ Another way to improve your self-confidence is dress nicely and keep yourself neatly groomed.

✓ Avoid distractions so that you complete tasks in order to build confidence.

✓ If your self-image is poor, then nothing you do in an outward sense will change that; you must begin to view yourself differently.

The Altitude of Your Attitude

Your attitude is critical. You must be very careful what you choose to think. A positive attitude is conducive to success. A negative attitude is not. If you are not now as successful as you'd like to be, maybe your own negative thinking and bad attitude are to blame. You can change. You can make your own good luck. Successful people don't sit at home waiting for the right opportunity or for adverse circumstances to change. They go out searching for opportunity. They trust their intuition. They take calculated risks. When they encounter circumstances not to their liking, they immediately set about changing those circumstances.

Part 1: The 4 Types of Attitude

There are 4 types of attitude that can we can adopt—and they are imperative in modeling and shaping a healthy and positive attitude.

The First Type of Attitude Is Ambition.

Those with an ambitious attitude make up the top 5% of people who know exactly what they want and are single-minded about success.

For these individuals failure is NOT an option! They always focus on things and situations from a positive point of view and are able to find the good in any predicament they may face.

They may even get to the point of being annoying to those around them because nothing seems to bother them! They don't rattle easily, and are quick to search for solutions when confronted with challenges instead of focusing on why something can't be done.

For those who are close to these ambitious individuals such as a good friend or spouse, it can be frustrating when something that they feel is a major problem seems little more than the latest issue to solve for them.

Persistence is a key ingredient for the ambitious person. Ambitious people know that achieving their goals won't be easy, but success rarely is. Just like failure is not an option, you have to tell yourself to keep working and working until you achieve your goals and dreams. Persistence is what allows you to do this in spite of any obstacles that get in the way.

The ambitious person always strives for lofty goals—you can't expect to be successful if you don't have high expectations of yourself. You must push to be better, smarter, stronger, faster, etc. than your competition—in school, in sports, in business and in life. Finding solutions to problems should be second nature, and when solutions are found to big problems, a lot of money can be made as a result!

The Second Type of Attitude Is Action.

Having an attitude of action is what allows you to get things done. *Ambition is the drive to do something, but it won't happen unless you get into action.*

Your success is directly proportionate to the amount of action you take:

- Massive action will yield massive results
- Minimal or no action will yield little or no results

In order to get into massive, effective action that will deliver to you the results you desire, you must have a carefully thought out plan that you continually work on. Every plan requires constant refinement; no plan was ever "perfect" from the beginning. The best plan can become obsolete in an instant due to unforeseen variables that affect the plan. Murphy's Law can show up and have a negative bearing on your plan in many different ways including changes in:

weather   finances   personnel   regulations   people

Any single variable can affect your "perfect" plan. Throwing multiple variables together can wreak total havoc. For this reason, *it is always prudent to be flexible in adjusting your plans*, and when applicable, have a "Plan B" or even a "Plan C" that will allow you to more rapidly adjust to a shifting landscape brought on by one or more uncontrollable variables.

Success likes speed, so get moving quickly toward obtaining the proper attitude and mindset with regard to your desired end result. You must be in constant action and not get trapped into thinking you cannot start until your plan is "done." It will never be "done." It might be "finished," as in, no longer being viable, but all plans will inevitably have mistakes that you will have to fix as you go. Waiting until everything is perfect will trap you in "inaction" as you refine and refine and refine . . .

Just get started!

The Third Type of Attitude Is Urgency.

A sure-fire way to get moving in the direction you need to go (or be driven!) is a sense of urgency. Time has a way of getting away from us, and as we get older, it seems to go by more quickly than in our earlier years. There is a reason for this that makes sense once it is brought to your attention.

When we are young, say . . . 12 years old, we may remember back to when we were perhaps 3 years old. Most of us can't remember what we were doing when we were 3 years of age, but for the sake of argument, let's say at the age of 12 we do. That gives us 9 years that we remember (12–3=9).

Now if we look at our current year of life at 12, it contains approximately 9 years of "stuff", or 1/9 of our total recorded and remembered events, memories, etc. *It therefore represents a rather large chunk in terms of its percentage of the total that we can recall—it comes out to about 11% of our total remembered experiences.*

This is an enormous percentage as you will see in a minute, and the first part of the reason why time seems to move more slowly at this age. Our current year of life at the age of 12 represents 11% of everything we have experienced up to that point in our lives, and many experiences are new and being done for the first time. This makes for more lasting memories as well. Almost no one forgets their "firsts" in life whether it is our first time riding a bike, our first kiss, getting our driver's license, etc.

Let's fast-forward now to 35 years of age. For the sake of argument, let's say that we can still recall back to what we were doing at the age of 3. *(More than likely it will be around 7, but more on that in a minute.)*

At 35 years old if we can still recall the 32 years between when we were 3 and our present age, that means that our current 35th year of life represents 1/32 of our total memories (35-3 = 32). *The percentage now drops way down to a mere 3% of what we have experienced up to this point as compared to the whopping 11% back when we were 12!* If we remember back to around 7 years of age, that still represents 1/28 of our total (35—7 = 28), or just 3.6% of our total recollections.

As we age, each passing year drops this percentage down lower and lower and the years seem to pass by more and more quickly. Each passing year represents smaller and smaller percentages of our total memories, and so as a result *our perception of time* appears to move it faster and faster. At the age of 70, if we can remember back to say, 10 years of age, that is a 60 year span of memories (70-10=60). Our current 70th year is a measly 1.7% of our total recollections. Maybe that's why as people age they move (and drive!) more slowly . . . they're trying to make each minute last as long as possible!

The preceding explanation does help you realize that time is indeed a very precious commodity for each and every one of us. Once it has passed by, we can never go back. Yesterday is history. *The only things that matter are the present and the future.* This doesn't mean you shouldn't learn from the past and history, but you cannot change it.

Every single person on this planet wakes up with the exact same amount in their "time bank." This "time bank" balance will be zero at the end of the day for everyone. It is up to each one of us to determine how to "spend" that amount. We each have 24 hours . . . 1440 minutes . . . 86,400 seconds to do something with in our lives each day. What are you going to do with the balance left in your "time bank" today?

One of the ways we can move ourselves along so that we waste as precious little time as possible is to set deadlines.

Deadlines have a way of creating that sense of urgency in us that gets us in action. It doesn't matter if it is a self-imposed deadline or one that is set for us due to some other limiting factor. Deadlines do what they are supposed to do, and that is to get us moving by developing that sense of urgency in us.

It is imperative that you also have the proper *confidence* to execute your plan. Expect to reach your lofty ambitions! Do not doubt that it is possible to succeed in whatever your endeavors may be. Have the right attitude and develop the habit of doing "it" anyway. Others may disagree with your methods. They may ridicule you because they do not share in your vision or agree with you. Remain steadfast and confident in your final outcome because only you can be the one to make your dreams a reality.

Setting realistic and achievable goals while stretching the bounds of what you think is possible are the best goals to have. Get a sense of clarity about what you hope to achieve and develop your sense of urgency so that you get things done . . . otherwise it is just as easy to say that you'll get to it "someday," and unfortunately, someday has a habit of turning into never.

The Fourth Type of Attitude Is Determination.

Being able to decide that you will persist until you succeed no matter what is the essence of determination. Persistence is the trait that helps drive our determination when the going gets tough. Having laser focus on your goals is also important in drawing you forward and helping you make the right decisions along the way.

Constantly hold up decisions and evaluate them in the context of, "Will this decision bring me closer to, or further away from my goals?" If you do this with every major decision you are faced with, it will help you tremendously in moving forward with achieving your goals.

You may have noticed that having the right attitude is a key ingredient in allowing us to achieve our goals or not. This is why we refer to goals and goal-setting frequently in this chapter. If you don't have clear, well-defined goals that are measurable and realistic, it will be next to impossible to achieve them. *(For more specific information about goal-setting, visit my site* http://

BestSuccessTraining.com *and sign up for your free account which includes many training modules on topics including attitude, mindset development, goal-setting and many others.)*

Determine what three things you will do every day in order to reach a particular goal that you have. If you don't have goals, or are unsure as to how to effectively create goals, it is imperative that you view my training on this topic. By having specific tasks to perform on a daily basis, you are creating a greater sense of determination because you are forcing yourself to do these tasks day after day after day . . .

Be specific in defining your daily tasks. If your goal is to make more sales of your product or service, set a specific goal each day of how many people you are going to contact that day and by what medium. For example, set a goal to contact 25 people by phone, 50 people by email, and make a post on three social media sites related to your product. Then commit to doing that every day without fail, don't stop until you have achieved your outcome and watch the magic happen! It's amazing what results you can get from consistent, determined and specific action . . . and it all starts with having the right attitude.

These 4 attitudes are at the root of all entrepreneurial success and are held by around 5% of all people. Of course, the 95% "others" also have ambitions and "want" things, but their ambitions are more like wishful thinking rather than specific goals with defined actions that are performed with Ambition, Action, Urgency and Determination.

Those in the 95% can be likened to sailors adrift on the sea of life without a rudder or compass to help steer them in the right direction. Because they don't have a plan and because they haven't chartered a specific course nor lined up a definite destination, they tend to drift with the tide. Sometimes they drift into undesirable ports. Sometimes their ship flounders and they end up as flotsam and jetsam floating with the tide.

If you are not now as successful as you'd like to be, now is the best time to set an ambitious but realistic goal, or series of progressive goals. Determine what three things you will do each day to reach a particular goal. Then simply do what you have determined to do, and don't stop until you have achieved your objective. This leads us to our next topic—developing a "never quit" attitude.

Part 2: Developing a "Never Quit" Attitude

One of the most important things you must do is develop a "never quit" attitude. It is imperative because we all have challenges to face. However it is how we deal with those challenges that will separate us from those who cannot adequately deal with them. Some things to keep in mind:

Everyone is faced with adversity.
Everyone is faced with hardship.
Everyone has to deal with unreasonable people.
Everyone has to deal with unplanned events.
Everyone has to deal with unexpected problems.
Everyone has to deal with unexpected expenses.
Everyone faces challenges at home.
Everyone faces challenges at work.
Everyone faces challenges dealing with family members.
Everyone faces challenges dealing with friends.

It is up to you to choose how to deal with these things as you go through life. You can simply give up and choose to ignore problems and challenges, or you can decide that you are going to meet them head on in order for you to succeed in whatever endeavor you are working on.

Remember that your attitude will determine your effectiveness in dealing with life's challenges. Your attitude shapes your thoughts and your actions. Having the proper attitude toward yourself, classmates, teammates, teachers, family, friends, clients, neighbors, distributors, vendors, etc. is absolutely a KEY ingredient that you must apply at all times! It's not always easy to maintain a positive attitude, especially in the face of incredible adversity or seemingly overwhelming odds. But, if you approach each challenge in turn with the right attitude, you can achieve ANYTHING!

One essential trait that you must harness is that of living more in harmony with yourself, other people and your environment. This is done by your thoughts, feelings, actions and attitude. When you achieve this, great things can happen for you.

So, how do you develop this "never quit" attitude when dealing with so many challenges, problems and unreasonable, non-supportive people?

Part 3: The Warrior Mindset

The warrior best exemplifies the "never quit" attitude that is being discussed here. Just like the samurai warriors of feudal Japan, you must also possess the mindset of someone who will not quit when faced with adversity.

In the simplest terms, the "Warrior Mindset" is a form of _mental discipline_ that enables those who have it to _face any challenge with grace and strength_. Those who possess it must _find a balance_ between being <u>passive</u> and <u>aggressive</u> in order to harness it's power effectively.

It is key to success both in business and in life for many reasons, and you will see exactly how to use it as a means of achieving your goals and dreams and for developing the proper attitude.

Throughout your life you face countless hurdles and obstacles that stand in your way. In every instance, you have a choice to make; do you turn back when you face the obstacle, or do you focus and commit to overcoming the obstacle. <u>This difference is the Warrior Mindset.</u>

Having this type of mindset will allow you to gain more discipline which is one key to <u>self-control</u>. It also helps you to find additional <u>courage</u> so you are not afraid to take action to solve your problems instead of avoiding them.

It also allows you to become more <u>persistent</u> and never give up when the going gets tough. Having the Warrior Mindset helps you to be more <u>patient</u>, knowing that things can take some time to develop, but not losing sight of your end result. You increase your <u>fortitude</u>—the ability to try again regardless of your previous failures. Knowing that you are making progress and learning <u>humility</u> and <u>harmony</u> helps you to work more effectively with others. This all helps <u>teamwork</u> and your ability to follow the proper path in all areas of your life.

For example, in your daily life, it is extremely important when dealing with your friends, boyfriend/girlfriend, or family that you have patience and harmony. In your interactions with your teachers, classmates, and co-workers, it is imperative that you have respect, motivation, discipline and fortitude in order to complete tasks and do your job.

Your mind is the most powerful force in the universe!

You can choose to believe that statement or not, but it is true, for nothing in this universe has ever happened without first existing in the mind. *It is the root of manifestation and holds the key to the Universe, for without the mind, there is nothing.* Think about it—every product, every discovery, every theory, every rule, everything that there is first had to be conceived of in the mind before it could be produced and brought into the physical world. It doesn't matter whether it is a table, a computer or a rocket, they all had to be thought of before they could be designed and built.

The mind of the Warrior should be clear and able to perceive their surroundings without distraction. It must be relaxed, yet alert; determined, yet unconcerned. This is the goal of the Warrior, and it must be your goal as well. Don't get bogged down in details, remember—ready, shoot, aim! Inaction is death—you must get into action, and massive action if you want to achieve massive results!

Once you are able to change your mindset and your attitude to one that is akin to a warrior's, you will begin to see barriers fall and obstacles disappear that you previously thought were impossible to overcome.

For a complete video training on the Warrior Mindset, visit http://BestSuccessTraining.com and join for free. You can also check out the preview video on our channel on YouTube here: https://www.youtube.com/watch?v=2SnPp5jDR24.

Part 4: Value-Driven Attitude Vs. Expectation-Driven Attitude

Value-Driven (Success) Attitude
vs.
Expectation-Driven (Failure) Attitude

In school, in business and in life, there are two dominant attitudes. The first is a *value-driven* attitude where we say "What can I do for you?" The other is an *expectation-driven* attitude where we say "What can you do for me?" Notice the difference? Are you operating from the first, value-oriented mindset? If so, success will follow, and will be proportional to the service and value that you provide. Greater value and service equals greater success, but the reverse is also true.

Those who adopt a value-driven attitude are always looking to see how they can deliver more. When people receive more value than they expect from you, your climb up the ladder of success has begun! This is one of those keys to success that many books on business and success preach. Delivering over and above what is expected of you, in school, in business and in life can bring you more quickly toward your end result.

If you are operating from the angle of trying to see what you can "get" out of a given situation or a person, your success will be limited. The reason is that once others see that you are only involved for yourself, they will distance themselves from you. Remember that your attitude and the way you approach every situation and every relationship will dictate your success or lack of it. Do not be afraid to take risks—you have to fail in order to succeed in many aspects of life. If you have an attitude that "failure is not an option" then you will be hesitant to take risks and that will in turn limit your results in what you are attempting to accomplish, both personally and professionally.

If you become involved in sales of any sort, view everyone with that attitude that they *need* what you *have*. If you view your prospects this way, not only will it make it easier for you to approach and talk to people, it will help you get over the fear of rejection. Remember that F.E.A.R. simply stands for False Evidence Appearing Real. It is what you make of it—nothing more. Be vigilant and dedicated to your success and you will experience more "luck" and "miracles" than you will believe possible!

Having an "attitude of gratitude" will begin to help you live a more harmonious life in balance and free of negativity. You must learn to appreciate the small as well as the large things in your life that you have reason to be grateful for. *Just having a bed to sleep in, a roof over your head, and food in your belly puts you ahead of the majority of people on this planet.* Half of the world's population lives on less than $2.50 per day, and 80% live on less than $10 per day. Many others struggle simply to survive day-to-day and spend much of their time hungry and uncertain of their future. Put this into perspective the next time you're doubting why you should be grateful for what you have.

It starts with having the right expectations for your outcome. If you don't have the right picture of what you want your ultimate, and I do mean ULTIMATE end result will be, nothing else you do will assist you in getting closer to it! Alternatively, if you have a crystal clear picture of what you want from your education, your life, your relationships, or your whatever, that picture will PULL you and DRAW you closer to it every day that you see it. This picture can be defined by what is on your goal board, your goal lists, or your daily affirmations and declarations, these things all pull us closer to our picture of our end result. For more information on these, visit http://BestSuccessTraining.com and sign up for your free membership.

Your current situation is only a culmination of all your past thoughts and actions, and is in NO WAY indicative of your future outcome.

Who we thought we were yesterday is who we are today.

Who we think we are today is who we will become tomorrow.

Why Attitude Is Everything

Your attitude is critical. You must be very careful what you choose to think. In simplest terms—a positive attitude is conducive to success, and a negative attitude is not. If you are not now as successful as you'd like to be, maybe your own negative thinking and bad attitude are to blame? If so, you can change. You can make your own "good luck".

Successful people don't sit at home waiting for the right opportunity or for adverse circumstances to change.

> They go out searching for opportunity.
> They trust their intuition.
> They take calculated risks.
> They don't let life "happen" to them.

When they encounter circumstances not to their liking, they immediately set about changing those circumstances.

Did you know that people who maintain a positive attitude produce 37% more income than those who do not? Think about it—just by consciously being more positive you can make more money!

There is a tremendous disparity between those with a positive attitude and those with a negative one. In general, people with positive attitudes tend to be more successful and earn more income than those with negative attitudes.

Perception of the world is how we see it consciously—if you have peace of mind, then you can choose to ignore the bad and focus on the good. If you put out powerful, positive thoughts, it will be difficult to have negative thoughts creep in. If something or someone is not congruent to your positive attitude and thoughts, then you need to remove it from your space.

Chapter 16 Checklist: The Altitude of Your Attitude

✓ A positive attitude is conducive to success. A negative attitude is not.

The 4 Types of Attitude

✓ The first type of attitude is *Ambition*. The person with this attitude focuses on things and situations from a positive point of view finds the good in any predicament they may face. Finding solutions to problems should be second nature.

✓ The second type of attitude is *Action*. Having an attitude of action is what allows you to get things done. Ambition is the drive to do something, but it won't happen unless you get into action.

✓ The third type of attitude is *Urgency*. A sure-fire way to get moving in the direction you need to go is a sense of urgency. One of the ways we can move ourselves along so that we waste as precious little time as possible is to set deadlines.

✓ The fourth type of attitude is *Determination*. Being able to decide that you will persist until you succeed no matter what is the essence of determination. Persistence is the trait that helps drive our determination when the going gets tough.

✓ Your attitude shapes your thoughts and your actions.

✓ If you approach each challenge in turn with the right attitude, you can achieve ANYTHING!

✓ You must form the "Warrior Mindset"—a form of mental discipline that enables those who have it to face any challenge with grace and strength.

✓ This allows you to become more persistent and never give up when the going gets tough. The Warrior Mindset helps you to be more <u>patient</u>, knowing that things can take some time to develop, but not losing sight of your end result. You increase your <u>fortitude</u>—the ability to try again regardless of your previous failures. Knowing that you are making progress and learning <u>humility</u> and <u>harmony</u> helps you to work more effectively with others. This all helps <u>teamwork</u> and your ability to follow the proper path in all areas of your life.

✓ In business and in life, there are two dominant attitudes.

- The first is a *value-driven* attitude where we say "What can I do for you?"
- The other is an *expectation-driven* attitude where we say "What can you do for me?"

✓ When people receive more value than they expect from you, your climb up the ladder of success has begun!

✓ Do not be afraid to take risks—you have to fail in order to succeed in many aspects of life and in business.

✓ Learn to appreciate the small as well as the large things in your life that you have reason to be grateful for.

✓ Who we thought we were yesterday is who we are today.

✓ Who we think we are today is who we will become tomorrow.

✓ People who maintain a positive attitude produce 37% more income than those who do not.

✓ Successful people don't sit at home waiting for the right opportunity or for adverse circumstances to change.

- They go out searching for opportunity.
- They trust their intuition.
- They take calculated risks.
- They don't let life "happen" to them.

✓ If something or someone is not congruent to your positive attitude and thoughts, then you need to remove it from your space.

CHAPTER 17

Health, Fitness & Avoiding the "Freshman 15"

Your health is of paramount importance; you only have one body, one temple that you must take care of. If you take care of yourself and stay in shape, you will be that much better prepared to deal with a threat to your personal safety. Whether you find yourself having to run away or physically defend yourself, if you are in good physical condition, you will have a better chance than if you are not.

Part 1: Sleep Habits

One of the easiest ways to improve or maintain your health is to ensure that you get enough sleep. Strive for at least 7–8 hours every night, and also try to go bed at the same time every night. You will fall asleep faster and wake up at the same time each morning feeling much more refreshed. In addition, your body will have a chance to heal itself, and your immune system will be able to function properly. Getting run down from a lack of sleep is a sure-fire way to get sick, and you cannot afford to get sick at college—you have too much to do!

Also, there is a misconception that you need to stay up late to get your work done, studying completed or projects finished. However, your productivity will be greater in the morning, so it is actually better to go to sleep earlier so you can get up earlier and maximize your productivity.

Now, there may be a problem with this because your roommate or others on your floor or in your building could stay up late, making noise and keeping you awake. Most college dorms have quiet hours, typically between 10pm—7am on school nights, and later on weekends. If those in your dorm are not adhering to those hours, contact your RA, student affairs or public safety office and let them know. These hours exist so that students can get the sleep they need.

Part 2: Proper Nutrition

Eating right is essential for maintaining proper health. What mom told you was true—breakfast is the most important meal of the day! After sleeping, your body has been burning calories, and you have an empty stomach when you wake up. Ignoring breakfast or simply having something to "hold you over" is doing your body and mind a disservice. Your body needs to refuel after resting, and making sure that you have a good breakfast will ensure that you get your metabolism going to produce the energy you need. You don't want to be distracted by a growling stomach in class and you will have trouble focusing on the work at hand. Long-term this will cause issues with both your health and your grades.

When you don't eat, it causes your body to store fat, so skipping breakfast to lose a few pounds will actually have the opposite effect! By eating and maintaining a healthy diet, you set yourself up for success because your body and mind will remain energized and focused on what needs to be done, instead of thinking about your next meal because you're hungry.

To keep your metabolism going and to feel fuller, eat smaller meals but eat more often. Limiting your food intake at each meal and controlling your portions is key to staying in shape and maintaining your health. Having smaller portions will allow you to eat more frequently, approximately every 2–3 hours, so that your body will always have food to convert to energy.

Every time you eat, you need to be smart about the mix of food that you consume. *Each meal should have a protein and a green vegetable.*

Proteins that are good for you include chicken, beef, fish, pork and eggs. These are the foods that increase your feeling of "fullness" and when you feel full, you will stop eating! Proteins are also key to building muscle, so if you are looking to get in shape, including a lot of protein in your diet is essential.

Increase the amount of salads and green vegetables in your diet such as spinach, broccoli, peppers and cucumbers. Limit your intake of starchy vegetables like corn and potatoes.

Another piece of the food mix are carbohydrates. They are important, but in moderation. Eat the majority of your carbs earlier in the day so that your body can use them for energy as the day progresses. If you eat carbs later in the day, there is a greater chance that they will be converted to fat.

Consuming whole grains is much preferred over processed grains such as white bread, one of the worst things you can eat. The same holds true for many other "white" foods including pasta and pizza, one of the staples of the hungry college student!

Fats are the final piece of the food matrix. Fats are essential, but in small quantities. They should be part of the food you eat, so check the amounts in what you are consuming to ensure that you are not ingesting too many saturated fats or too many fats overall.

The ideal meal portion mix is easy to follow simply by using your hand. You should have 4–6 oz of protein (size of your palm), ½ to 1 cup of carbs (size of your fist), 1 to 1 ½ cups of vegetables (2 fists), and 1 tablespoon of fats (size of the top of your thumb). If you follow this mix, you will give your body the best mix of foods for your optimal health.

Make sure that you also drink enough water and stay hydrated. Drinking a lot of water will also ensure that you digest your food properly and will also help you feel full—plus it has no calories! Drinking sodas and sports drinks which contain lots of sugars just cause you to ingest empty calories.

Some sample meal plans include the following:

1. Breakfast
   a) Eggs (omelet with turkey, broccoli, spinach & cheese)
   b) Oatmeal or whole grain toast with peanut butter
2. Snack #1 (choose one)
   a) Yogurt
   b) Handful of almonds or cashews
   c) Small piece of fruit

3. Lunch
   a) Chicken, pork, turkey or beef
   b) Green beans, mixed vegetables or salad
   c) Brown rice
4. Snack #2 (choose one)
   a) Yogurt
   b) Handful of almonds or cashews
   c) Small piece of fruit
5. Dinner
   a) Chicken, pork, turkey or beef
   b) Large serving of green vegetables

Part 3: Physical Fitness

Maintaining physical fitness throughout not just your college years, but your entire life should be a goal that everyone has. Unfortunately, it is much easier to *not* maintain good fitness because it takes *work and effort* to stay fit and healthy. However, the rewards of maintaining good physical fitness and health throughout your life are worth it. It will manifest in your feeling and performing better as well as lowering medical costs and ultimately help you live a longer life.

As already discussed, proper nutrition and diet is one of the most important aspects to maintaining health. The other side of that equation is staying physically fit. This allows all of your body's systems to work optimally—cardiovascular, skeletal, muscular, digestive, immune, nervous, lymphatic, urinary, respiratory, endocrine, integumentary (skin) and reproductive.

The topic of physical fitness in terms of workout routines and other specifics is well beyond the scope of this book. However, there are some broad general statements we can make that will serve as a guide and hopefully motivate you to learn more specific information and find what works best for you.

First and foremost, your physical health begins with your *mental health*. If you have a poor understanding and attitude toward physical fitness, it will be a hindrance to you improving yourself. Having a positive attitude toward fitness and health will help get you moving. The previous chapter on attitude can help you in this regard.

Cardiovascular health can be improved by increasing your heart rate through various exercises including walking, jogging, and bike riding, or by using a treadmill, stepper or elliptical machine. Other activities that enable you to learn while you work out include kickboxing, boxing, and martial arts training. These are more useful than simply running in place!

These activities will force your cardiovascular system to work harder by increasing your heart rate and blood circulation. Cardiovascular workouts will also burn calories, but are not the best for fat loss. In fact, the production of the fat burning hormone, leptin, actually decreases for up to 24–48 hours after an intense cardio workout!

Your heart is a muscle, and if you don't exercise it, the heart will get weaker. Regular cardio workouts strengthen the heart and keep it healthy. It also boosts your metabolism which speeds up other processes in your body so that it becomes easier to maintain your weight. Cardio workouts also cause your body to release endorphins, your "feel good" hormone. This will lower your stress levels and contribute to better overall health. Additionally, better cardiovascular health helps you recover faster from your workouts because your body gets the oxygen it needs more quickly. Your muscles won't be as sore after a workout and it assists the muscles in rebuilding and repairing themselves more rapidly.

In order to stimulate production of this fat-burning hormone, leptin check out http://news.harvard.edu/gazette/story/2002/02/hormone-leptin-tied-to-fat-breakdown-in-muscle/. You need to perform **muscle-building** exercises that involve multiple muscle groups instead of isolation exercises that only target one or two specific muscles.

Exercises such as squats, lunges, dead lifts and squat thrusts all invoke core muscles as well as the larger muscles in the legs and glutes. Doing exercises for your upper body that simultaneously invoke multiple muscle groups such as bench press, pull-ups and push-ups work your arms, back, chest and shoulders and will also allow you to see faster results. Go for more volume, meaning sets x reps x weight. High Intensity Interval Training (HIIT) also helps. These types of exercises will actually stimulate the production of testosterone and leptin in your body for 24–48 hours, meaning that your body will continue to burn fat even after your workout and when you're sleeping!

Do your own research and figure out what exercises make the most sense for your individual situation. Get in the habit of doing them on a consistent basis. Working out several days each week on a consistent schedule is the key to seeing results. Switching up the exercises that you do is another important aspect to continually moving forward and closer to your fitness goals. Don't do the same old routine for months; you will plateau and not be able to move any further along in your fitness pursuit.

Part 4: Healthy Hygiene

Another critical point to helping you stay healthy is basic hygiene. Things such as frequent hand washing, and covering your nose and mouth when coughing and sneezing are simple things that are easy to do to help keep both you and others from getting sick. On a college campus, there are thousands of people on a daily basis that are all touching the same door handles, lab equipment, and remote controls to name just a few items. They all contain countless germs that threaten your health and well-being.

It is vitally important to make smart decisions about what and who you come in contact with each day. Keep your hands away from your eyes, nose and mouth. Frequently wash your hands and take advantage of hand sanitizer in order to kill germs. It is a good idea to have a small bottle of hand sanitizer in your backpack or purse so you can clean your hands any time you want or need to.

Refrain from touching things you don't need to, or be smarter about how to do. For example, when opening a door or holding it open, use the back of your hand or your forearm instead of your hand to minimize contact with outside surfaces. Use your knuckle to press the elevator button instead of your fingertip. These habits you form with regard to improving your hygiene will have a direct, positive impact on your health not just in college, but for your entire life.

If your roommate is sick, be diligent about cleaning surfaces after they have touched them. For example, wipe the faucets before brushing your teeth after them, or use a patch of toilet paper to handle the faucet or to flush the toilet. These small details can go a long way—so don't ignore them if you want to proactively maintain good health.

College can be stressful as pressures mount related to assignments, term papers, projects, lab reports and other responsibilities related to school. In addition, there may be additional pressures from girlfriends/boyfriends, parents, friends, roommates and others. Increased levels of stress contribute to a decline in immune system function, leaving you more vulnerable to getting run down and sick.

It is important to manage your stress in college and in life. You need to find activities that allow you to forget about these stresses. Joining a club, being part of a team, or engaging in consistent workouts are all conducive to helping you manage your stress during this often stressful time in your life.

Chapter 17 Checklist: Health, Fitness & Avoiding the "Freshman 15"

✓ Your physical health begins with your *mental health.* Having a positive attitude toward fitness and health will help get you moving.

✓ If you take care of yourself and stay in shape, you will be that much better prepared to deal with a threat to your personal safety.

✓ One of the easiest ways to improve or maintain your health is to ensure that you get enough sleep. Strive for 7–8 hours at the same time each night.

✓ Eating right is essential for maintaining proper health. Following a healthy diet sets you up for success because your body and mind will remain energized and focused on what needs to be done and not on food.

✓ Eat a balanced diet of proteins, lots of green vegetables, and whole grains.

✓ The rewards of maintaining good physical fitness and health throughout your life will manifest in your feeling and performing better as well as lowering medical costs and ultimately help you live a longer life.

✓ Regular cardio workouts strengthen the heart and keep it healthy.

✓ Working out several days each week on a consistent schedule is the key to seeing results.

✓ Frequent hand washing, and covering your nose and mouth when coughing and sneezing are simple things that are easy to do to help keep both you and others from getting sick.

✓ Increased levels of stress contribute to a decline in immune system function, leaving your more vulnerable to getting run down and sick.

✓ Find activities that allow you to forget about these stresses.

Safety Tips for Women

Women have a unique set of safety challenges, and this chapter includes information specific to certain tips and habits they can develop to increase their personal safety and security. Some of the information included in this chapter comes from interviewing prisoners who were incarcerated due to various crimes including sexual assault and rape.

Statistics show that one in every four women in America will be sexually assaulted in her lifetime. Every 15 seconds a woman is beaten by her boyfriend or husband. In the USA, every two minutes a woman is raped, and 78% of those were assaulted by someone they knew. Incredibly, a survey revealed that 50% of Canadian women have experienced an incident of sexual assault or physical violence in their lives. In Australia, 19% of women aged 18 to 24 experienced an act of violence during the past year. These are SHOCKING statistics!

Realize that many sexual assaults are committed by someone that the victim knows. You need to recognize the progression of violence as it is occurring. It starts with the "look", then verbal cues and suggestive language and finally the attack.

Self-Defense Tips for Women

The following information can help any woman increase their chances of survival. Much of this information has been taken from studies as well as by surveying inmates in prison to help determine how they go about choosing their victims.

Ladies, just one tip from this section could save your life!

For almost 20 years I have been teaching martial arts as well as specialized self-defense classes for women and other groups. During that time I have taught many women how to protect and look after themselves. Since most women fear attacks of a sexual nature more than anything else, most of the following tips are geared toward that. If you are a woman, the following is a list of things that will increase your safety. *Remember that violence is chaotic and is not a game.* <u>There is no "tapping out" like in a training or sport environment.</u>

1. Trust your instincts. Women are very intuitive. If you think a situation might be dangerous then it probably is. That feeling you are getting should be trusted rather than ignored.

2. Rape and other sexual assault is always a risk. If you find yourself under assault, use the techniques in this book and your body's natural weapons such as your fingernails to gouge your attacker's face and arms. It will mark them for identification and you will have DNA under your nails for investigators.

3. Drive your vehicle in a courteous manner. Nobody appreciates rude hand signs, laying on the horn, etc. Remember that you will eventually have to stop, even if it is to refuel. You may be followed for many miles by someone that wants to "teach you a lesson" because you made yourself a target to them.

4. Wearing revealing clothing will ensure that you attract plenty of attention from everyone—good and bad. You want to look good, but be smart about your clothing choices and cognizant of where you will be and how you will appear.

5. Drinking excessive amounts of alcohol, taking mind altering drugs and leaving ANY food or drink unattended is a recipe for disaster. Be smart with your alcohol intake, and never leave your food or drink unattended where it may be tampered with without your knowledge.

6. NEVER pick up hitch-hikers and ABSOLUTELY NEVER hitch-hike yourself.

7. If you live alone, it is a good idea to make sure that all your mail is addressed to you by just your first initial followed by your surname. Never allow mail to be addressed to you with salutations like Miss, Mrs, Ms. or with your first name. Letters and parcels pass many eyes before they get to you. Make them nondescript as to your sex and

marital status. Why allow anybody even one extra shred of information about you?

8. NEVER walk alone at night or at any time in isolated areas. Predators love these—avoid them.

9. Many forced sexual acts are committed by people who the victims knew, or at least, thought they knew! Be friendly and polite by all means but be aware of tell-tale signs of "strange" behavior. Be firm about any unwanted attention, particularly in the work place.

10. Sexual attack is usually preceded by some visual sign, which is usually preceded by some verbal approach before the physical action. Recognize the sequence: the look—the talk—the attack.

11. Your elbow is the strongest point on your body—if you are close enough to use it, do!

12. If you are a victim of a robbery, and the robber asks you for your wallet or purse, do not hand it to them! Instead, throw it away from you and chances are they are more interested in it than you. When they go for it, run away as fast as possible in the opposite direction! Kick off your heels to run faster!

13. If you are ever kidnapped or captured and thrown in the trunk of a car, kick out the tail lights and stick your arm out the hole! The driver will not see you, but everybody else will.

14. As soon as you get into your car, lock the doors and drive away. Do not make a call, send a text, eat a snack, write a list, etc. Chances are that if a predator has been watching you, they will attempt to get into your car after you open it to get in and before you drive away.

15. Before getting in your car, look around you and also look into your car including the passenger side floor and the back seats to make sure no one is there. Also look at the vehicles parked next to you on all sides and notice if there is anyone sitting alone in a vehicle parked next to yours. If so, you may want to walk back the way you came and have someone walk you to your vehicle. Better safe than sorry!

16. If you get into your car and there is already someone in it, do not drive away if you are instructed to do so! Instead, drive into anything and although you may wreck your

car, your air bag will save you but chances are not your attacker. If they are in the back seat, it will be even worse for them. Immediately get out of the car and run!

17. If you are parked next to a van that is on the driver's side of your car, get in the passenger side! Most serial killers attack their victims by pulling them into a van while the women are trying to get into their cars. Stay safe and fool your would-be kidnapper!

18. Always take the elevator instead of the stairs—staircases are perfect places to be caught alone and a perfect crime spot.

19. If your attacker has a gun and you are not under their control, RUN away in a zig-zag pattern. Statistics show that they will only have about a 4% chance of hitting you, and even if they do, the chances of hitting a vital organ are even smaller.

20. Women tend to be more sympathetic than men—don't be! It may get you raped or killed! Serial killers can be well-educated, good-looking and able to play on the sympathies of unsuspecting women such as walking with a limp or using a cane, asking for help, etc.

21. If you hear strange or unusual sounds coming from your front door of your home, do NOT open the door! There have been reports of a crying baby, a woman asking for help, etc. Call for help if you believe there to be a real problem. Do NOT get tricked into opening a locked door! There were reports several years ago of a serial killer that used the recorded sound of a baby crying to get people to open their door, thinking a baby was outside needing help. This was reported by multiple, single women and was even reported during an episode of *America's Most Wanted*. Don't think it cannot happen to you—it can.

A Group of Rapists and Date Rapists in Prison Were Interviewed on What They Look for in a Potential Victim

Here are some interesting facts:

1. The first thing men look for in a potential victim is hairstyle. They are most likely to go after a woman with a

ponytail, bun, braid or other hairstyle that can easily be grabbed. They are also likely to go after a woman with long hair. Women with short hair are not common targets.

2. The second thing men look for is clothing. They will look for women with clothing that is easy to remove quickly. Many of them carry scissors or knives specifically to cut clothing.

3. They also look for women on their cell phone, searching through their purse or doing other activities while walking because they are off guard and can be easily overpowered.

4. Men are most likely to attack & rape in the early morning, between 5:00am and 8:30am.

5. The number one place women are abducted from/attacked is grocery store parking lots. Number two is office parking lots/garages. Number three is public restrooms.

6. The thing about these men is that they are looking to grab a woman and quickly move her to another location where they don't have to worry about getting caught.

7. Only 2% of criminals who were interviewed said they carried weapons because rape carries a 3–5 year sentence but rape with a weapon is 15–20.

8. If you put up any kind of a fight at all, they get discouraged because it only takes a minute or two for them to realize that going after you isn't worth it because it will be time-consuming.

9. These men said they would not pick on women who have umbrellas, or other similar objects that can be used from a distance, in their hands. Keys are not a deterrent because you have to get really close to the attacker to use them as a weapon. So, the idea is to convince these guys you're not worth it.

10. Several defense mechanisms are: If someone is following behind you on a street or in a garage or with you in an elevator or stairwell, look them in the face and ask them a question, like "What time is it?" or make general small talk: "I can't believe it is so cold out here", or "We're in for a bad winter." Now that you've seen their face and could identify them in a line-up; you lose appeal to them as a target.

11. If someone is coming toward you, hold out your hands in front of you and yell "STOP!" or "STAY BACK!" Most

rapists said they'd leave a woman alone if she yelled or showed that she would not be afraid to fight back. Again, they are looking for an EASY target.

12. If you carry pepper spray (a VERY good idea,) yell "I HAVE PEPPER SPRAY" and hold it out as a deterrent.

13. If someone grabs you, you can't beat them with strength but you can by outsmarting them. If you are grabbed around the waist from behind, pinch the attacker either under the arm (between the elbow and armpit) OR in the upper inner thigh—VERY VERY HARD. Try pinching yourself in those places as hard as you can stand it; it hurts!

14. After the initial hit, always go for the GROIN. If you slap or punch a guy's private parts it is extremely painful. You might think that you'll anger the guy and make him want to hurt you more, but the thing these rapists said is that they want a woman who will not cause a lot of trouble. Start causing trouble, and he's out of there. You can also drop to the ground and grab the man around his leg by wrapping your arms around his leg—he can not walk or get you off of him as you scream. Try this with your husband or boyfriend to see how well it works.

15. When the guy puts his hands up to you, grab his first two fingers and bend them back as far as possible with as much pressure pushing down on them as possible.

16. Of course, other things we hear still apply. Always be aware of your surroundings, take someone with you if you can, and if you see any odd behavior, don't dismiss it, go with your instincts! You may feel a little silly at the time, but you'd feel much worse if the guy really was trouble.

Chapter 18 Checklist: Safety Tips for Women

✓ One in four women in America will be sexually assaulted in her lifetime.

✓ Every 15 seconds a woman is beaten by her boyfriend or husband.

✓ Recognize the following progression:

- the look
- verbal cues
- suggestive language
- physical touching
- actual attack

✓ Trust your instincts; if something feels wrong, it probably is.
✓ Avoid consuming excessive amounts of alcohol or take drugs. When you are impaired, you cannot defend yourself as effectively as when you are sober.
✓ Do not walk alone in dark or dimly lit areas if at all possible.
✓ If you are robbed, throw your wallet or purse away from the attacker so they have to get it. When they do you can make your escape.
✓ Drive away as soon as you get into your car—do not check your messages, text, make a call, etc. Get in and go.
✓ Be firm about any unwanted attention, particularly in the work place.
✓ Your elbow is the strongest point on your body—use it!
✓ Look at the vehicles parked next to you on all sides and notice if there is anyone sitting alone in a vehicle parked next to yours.
✓ Most attacks & rapes occur in the early morning, between 5:00am and 8:30am.
✓ Most rapists said they'd leave a woman alone if she yelled or showed that she would not be afraid to fight back.

CHAPTER 19

Prevention and Post-Altercation

Part 1: Prevention

Throughout our lives most humans try to avoid conflict. We reason, make excuses, lie, blame . . . we will do almost anything in an effort to avoid conflict. However, there are times when nothing we do works, and conflict erupts around us or to us.

As previously stated, the number one most important thing you can do to prevent becoming a victim of a physical confrontation is awareness of your surroundings—people, places and things. Simply having the foresight to be able to detect a potential conflict with a certain person or due to a certain situation or position can go a long way toward avoiding a problem. Be cognizant of your most accessible escape route wherever you may be—home, work, movies, mall, etc. Make it a habit to notice emergency exits and alternate ways of leaving an area, especially when you are entering an unfamiliar area or building.

Being armed with awareness™, preparation and training can go a long way to securing your personal safety when things just aren't working out the way you had hoped. When this point of no return happens, it is your duty to spring into action and let your training take over. *If you think about it too long, your chances of success shrink dramatically.*

Part 2: Post-Altercation

Immediately after an altercation we may find ourselves alive, but wounded along with anyone else we may be with. Assess the extent of your injuries and the injuries of anyone else before proceeding. Stem hemorrhaging of major wounds with pressure and any available clean clothing such as a t-shirt, scarf, socks, etc. *Minor cuts and bruises should not take any of your attention in the critical seconds and minutes immediately following an altercation that causes injury.* Stabilize any suspected broken bones, but do NOT move any victim with a head or neck injury since moving them may make the injury worse.

Call 9–1-1 immediately after stabilizing the injured if any exist and be prepared to report your position. If you are an unfamiliar area, look for street signs or major landmarks that may assist emergency personnel in finding you as soon as possible.

If you have not already eliminated the threat, try to immobilize them by tying them up. Use belts, suspenders, shoelaces, etc. to secure your attacker(s) until help arrives.

Counseling may be needed or required after a violent encounter—especially for children. Seek grief counseling if anyone was critically wounded or killed. If someone was lost, honor their memory by remembering their life, not their death.

Part 3: Living in the Aftermath

You will surely have a range of emotions and feelings that may seem to be too much to bear after an encounter. It is important to recognize these and verbalize or write down what they are. Depending upon what actually transpired, either you were successful or you were not successful with regard to the outcome of the conflict. You may feel angry, sad, worried, afraid or calm, out of control or in control, outraged, scared, powerless or powerful, etc. Make sure that you share your feelings with someone—anyone after the event whether it is a friend, family member, or professional.

It is important that you try to understand what happened and maybe even why it happened, as well as remembering that you survived, even if others did not. There may be a reason or there may not. Don't even put thoughts out there such as "why them, not me?" or "it should have been me, not them" or "they didn't deserve it" etc.

Don't feel like it was your fault, but do accept some responsibility for what occurred. Perhaps you have been under a lot of pressure lately. Maybe things in your life were making you not feel or act like yourself. There may be that something about you or your demeanor that could have been a spark that helped trigger the attack. Try to identify if there was anything you are aware of that could have caused events to unfold as they did. Chances are there was nothing you could have done to prevent it, but analyze everything you possibly can in an attempt to understand it.

The hours, days, weeks, months and even years after a violent encounter can change lives forever. The innocence that was felt prior to a life-altering event is gone, many times replaced with a harder, colder view of life in general.

There is often no reason for random violence—it could be induced by personal tragedy, drugs, desperation, hunger, etc. Human beings are normally social animals—we usually get along. However, there are also those who shun society or who have a difficult time adjusting to it, such as a newly released prisoner from jail.

All we can do is "keep on keeping on" the best we can, and honor the memories of those we have lost in ways that would make them proud of us with the time we have left in our own lives.

Chapter 19 Checklist: Prevention and Post-Altercation

✓ Most humans try to avoid conflict, but conflict may erupt around us or to us.

✓ Be cognizant of your most accessible escape route wherever you may be.

✓ Notice emergency exits and alternate ways of leaving any area, especially unfamiliar ones.

✓ When you are left with no choice but to act, it is your duty to spring into action and let your training take over and do whatever it takes to survive.

✓ After an altercation, assess the extent of your injuries and the injuries of anyone else before proceeding.

✓ Call 9–1–1 and be prepared to give your location.

✓ Seek grief counseling if anyone was critically wounded or killed.

✓ Make sure that you share your feelings with someone—anyone after the event whether it is a friend, family member, or professional.

✓ Don't feel like it was your fault, but do accept some responsibility for what occurred.

✓ There is often no reason for random violence.

10 step report on how to avoid Facebook Cyber-Bullying:
http://www.wikihow.com/Stop-Bullying-on-Facebook
Facebook Bullying Resource for Parents, Teens and Educators
https://www.facebook.com/safety/bullying
Adult Bullying Reference:
https://nobullying.com/adult-bullying/
Reporting Abuse on Facebook:
https://www.facebook.com/help/1417189725200547
Twitter On-line Abuse Link:
https://support.twitter.com/articles/15794#
Instagram On-line Abuse Link:
https://help.instagram.com/527320407282978
Date Rape reference:
https://www.womenshealth.gov/publications/our-publications/fact
-sheet/date-rape-drugs.html#h
Teen Sexual Assault Reference:
https://www.victimsofcrime.org/help-for-crime-victims/get-help
-bulletins-for-crime-victims/bulletins-for-teens/sexual-assault
What to do if you are victim or Dating Violence:
http://healthcenter.ucsc.edu/shop/sadv/dating-violence.html
Information, statistics and more including a dating violence quiz:
http://www.NationalSave.org

US and World Travel Safety Maps & Resources

Global Travel Warnings:
http://www.nationsonline.org/oneworld/travel_warning.htm
https://travel.state.gov/content/passports/en/alertswarnings.html
Mexico Travel Warnings:
http://www.travelweekly.com/uploadedFiles/MEXICOMAP4.pdf

APPENDIX B

SAFETY FORMS AND CHECKLISTS

Performing an online search will reveal countless websites that contain lots of information for you—but the results can be overwhelming! The following are some of the best online resources for helping you further educate yourself on various aspects of personal safety as well as emergency and disaster planning. Make use of them and stay safe!

http://www.homesecurity.org/checklists/personal-safety-checklist/
http://checklist.com/personal-security-checklist/
http://www.realsimple.com/home-organizing/organizing/home-safety
-checklist
http://www.redcross.org/prepare/disaster-safety-library
https://www.usfa.fema.gov/downloads/pdf/home_safety_checklist.pdf
https://www.state.gov/m/ds/rls/rpt/19773.htm
https://safetyrisk.net/free-safety-checklists/
http://thesafetylibrary.com/lib/safetyforms/safetyforms.php
http://www.lionsclubs.org/resources/EN/pdfs/personal_safety_checklist
.pdf

Emergency Preparedness 72-Hour Kit
(minimum recommended by the *American Red Cross*)

Heavy Duty Backpack	Work Gloves & Bandana
LifeStraw water filter (1000 liters)	Hygiene Kit (TP, deodorant, wipes)
Battery powered radio	Cell Phone, Whistle & Compass
Battery powered flashlight	Light Sticks & Hand/Foot warmers
Emergency Blanket & Rain Poncho	Sturdy Knife (full tang preferred)
Food bars / Protein bars	Extra Batteries & Chargers
Duct tape & Plastic Sheeting	Personal Items (medication, etc.)
Dust mask (N95 rated)	First Aid Kit

Dear Reader,

I hope that you have enjoyed reading and learning from *The Ultimate Guide to College Safety.* Refer to it often as you become more familiar and comfortable with the information and continue your (safe) journey through college and beyond . . . look for our related safety app, *Safety STAT,* coming soon to *iTunes* and *Google Play* store.

It is my sincere wish that you never need to put into practice any of the physical self-defense techniques in this guide, but should you find yourself in a situation that requires you to act, do so without hesitation and commit your entire being to the successful outcome of the situation so that you can live to enjoy another day.

The more you are aware, learn and practice, the more comfortable you will become and the more likely you will stay safe during your college years.

Look for our other books including (links go to books on *Amazon*):

- Self-Defense Survival Guide: How To Survive When You're Fighting For Your Life
- Corrections Officer Knife Attack Survival Course
- College Campus Safety Officer Defensive Tactics Training Course
- The Altitude Of Your Attitude

Good Luck and Stay Safe!

Master Peter J. Canavan
President, *North American Hapkido Tae Kwon Do Federation*
Owner, *PJC Services—Information Technology & Web Solutions*
Public Safety Officer, *Wilkes University*
Act 235 Lethal Weapons Certified Agent (Pennsylvania)
Twitter: @pjcpete / Facebook: facebook.com/pjcpete

YouTube: https://www.youtube.com/user/BestSuccess
   Training
Email: MasterPete@LearnSelfDefenseOnline.com
websites: http://www.LearnSelfDefenseOnline.com
http://PeteCanavan.com | http://www.htkdi.com |
   http://www.nahtf.com
http://CampusSafetyUniversity.com | http://GuideTo
   CollegeSafety.com

Be Aware—Be Prepared—Be Safe!

APPENDIX C

PRESSURE POINT AND STRIKE CHARTS - FRONT

EYES

UNDER CHEEKBONES

EARS

JAW (MANDIBULAR NERVE)

UPPER LIP (PHILTRUM)

GUM LINE (MANDIBLE)

PHARYNX (ADAM'S APPLE)

NECK (JUGULAR AND CAROTID)

THROAT (SUPRESTERNAL FOSSA)

. BEHIND COLLARBONE

. INNER ELBOW (RADIAL NERVE)

. OUTER ELBOW (ULNAR NERVE)

. FOREARM

. INNER WRIST (RADIAL NERVE)

. OUTER WRIST (ULNAR NERVE)

. ARMPIT (AXILLA)

. SOLAR PLEXUS (XIPHOID PROCESS)

. RIBS (7TH INTERCOSTAL SPACE)

. FLOATING RIB (11TH RIB)

. BELLY (URINARY BLADDER)

. TESTES

. INGUINAL CREASE (INNER GROIN)

. INSIDE OF THIGH

. INSTEP (BETWEEN 2ND AND 3RD METATARSAL)

. INNER ANKLE (RIGHT ABOVE BONE)

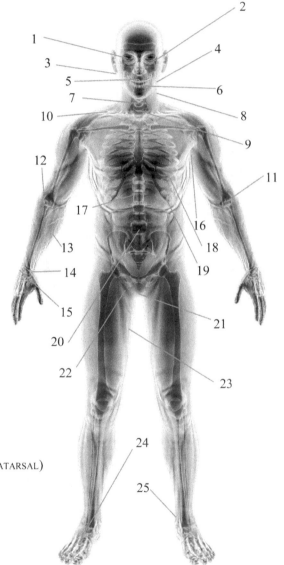

PRESSURE POINT AND STRIKE CHARTS - BACK

1.BEHIND THE EARS (MASTOID PROCESS)
2. BACK OF NECK (TRAPEZIUS MUSCLE)
3. HEART (1ST - 4TH THORACIC VERTEBRAE)
4. TRICEPS
5. KIDNEYS (3RD-5TH LUMBAR VERTEBRAE)
6. WEB BETWEEN FINGERS
7. WEB BETWEEN THUMB AND INDEX FINGER
8. FINGERS
9. BACK OF KNEE
10. INSIDE OF KNEE
11. INSIDE OF ANKLE
12. BACK OF ANKLE (ACHILLES TENDON)

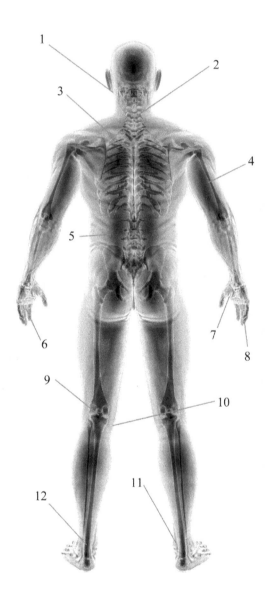

ACKNOWLEDGMENTS

To my wife, Susan, who has never wavered in her patience and support of me and my many endeavors. She is the glue that holds our family together and I love her dearly. Thank you!

To my three sons—Austin, Carson and Pierson; you have been the inspiration behind wanting to keep both you and others safe and secure, not only at college, but for the rest of your lives. You are the best sons a father could ever hope for and I am proud of you all.

To my father, the late Dr. John Peter Canavan—the most intelligent and genuine person I have ever known. You continue to inspire every word that I write, and I wish you could read this. I miss you, Dad.

To my mother, Russetta the Librarian. My love of reading and writing came from you and that is something truly invaluable. Thank you for nurturing my interest in reading and for helping edit this work.

To my sisters, Theresa and Dolores for their insights and assistance with this book. Although we may live far apart, we remain close.

To my good friend, David Jolley for his proof-reading and editing assistance with this book—thanks, Dave!

To my friends Mary Jo and D.L. Sadvary—thank you so much for your valuable insights into dorm room security as parents of college students. What you shared with me is included and will help many other students.

To the *Wilkes University* students who read and critiqued this manuscript. For your invaluable insights into this material, a BIG thank you goes out to: Alexandra Giammanco, Cody Morcom, Paige Thomas, Alyssa Alfano, Larissa Ressler, Sarah Kennedy, Tina Krug, Katy Ferry, Gabby Molitoris, Sarah Hughes, Shane Bleicherotto, Alexis Morgan and Kevin Abraham. You guys and girls rock!

A very special "Thank You!" to Tom Mooney for his professional work taking the high-quality pictures and shooting the videos for this work.

To Master Vincent J. Sperduto to whom I owe my martial arts and self-defense skills. Thank you for everything!

Author Pete Canavan has worked as a university public safety officer and is familiar with many of the safety challenges facing college students as a result of first-hand experience. He has also studied the martial arts and taught self-defense for over 20 years to men, women and children of all ages.

Pete is passionate about helping others improve their personal safety. He speaks and conducts seminars for schools, businesses, security and law enforcement, bartenders & bouncers, students, businesses, realtors and private citizens.

Pete has owned and operated his own information technology company, *PJC Services*, since 1995. He holds a Bachelor of Science in *Computers & Information Systems* and a minor in *Marketing* from King's College in Wilkes-Barre, PA.

His clients cover a wide variety of vertical markets including retail, legal, manufacturing, medical and education. His company also develops and hosts websites ranging from basic informational sites to secure database-driven e-commerce shopping sites. Pete's expertise with information technology keeps his clients' sites and systems secure. This book includes many best practices with regard to keeping your computers and other devices secure. It also contains vital information about securing your social media accounts and how to keep your identity from being stolen.

Master Pete has authored several books, training and continuing education programs designed for Department of Corrections Officers (*Corrections Officer Knife Attack Self-Defense Training Course*) and Campus Public Safety Officers (*College Campus Safety Officer Defensive Tactics Course*). These programs educate officers in the field on how to remain safe in a tough work environment. They are for public safety officers, law enforcement and other officers and provide information regarding self-defense, restraint techniques and weapons defenses. *The Self-Defense Survival Guide* is a guide to physical safety and personal protection and is perfect for anyone looking to improve both their physical and mental self-defense skills.

Another book, *The Altitude Of Your Attitude* in the personal development space stresses the importance of attitude on achieving success. Information from that book is included.

Pete has written articles for various periodicals, both on-line and off-line. He has been interviewed by nationwide radio programs in relation to his expertise on self-defense and personal safety.

Master Pete has studied many styles of marital arts. He holds official certifications from the *World Hapkido Federation*, the *United States TaeKwonDo Council*, the *North American Hapkido TaeKwonDo Federation*, and *Nippon Kobodo Jikishin-Kai USA*.

Master Pete is an expert with many martial arts weapons. He is also an *Act 235 Lethal Weapons Certified Agent* and is proficient with many types of firearms. In addition, Pete is certified in First Aid, CPR and AED use. He lives in Northeast Pennsylvania with his wife and three sons.

Author Pete Canavan has dedicated the past 20 years of his life helping keep his students and clients safe from all manner of online and offline threats. Pete is available for speaking, consulting, training, article writing and legal testimony. To learn more, visit PeteCanavan.com for information on media interviews including a complete media kit, links to past interviews, and one-sheets. Pete's latest media appearances as well as recent interviews can also be found there.

CPSIA information can be obtained
at www.ICGtesting.com
Printed in the USA
BVHW071108130219
540160BV00028B/2144/P